To Julie
with best wishes
for great success and
happiness
Carol A. Walker

WAKE UP AMERICA

REGAIN YOUR AMERICAN HERITAGE

Become Financially Fit Through Debt Elimination

BY JOHN RIVERA, PH.D. & CAROL WALKER

BOOK DEDICATION

We would like to dedicate this book to Kimberly, Kevin, Kelly and Jesse, as well as our friends, family, and community who have given so much to us. A special acknowledgment to those who have come before us and worked so faithfully to give us this opportunity to fulfill America's potential.

Published by Financial Freedom Enterprises
180 N. Woodruff
Idaho Falls, ID 83403, U.S.A.

First published May 1997

ISBN 0 9657857 0 5

Table of Contents

Due to the urgency of publication deadlines, Dr. Rivera was not involved in the selection of illustrations and final editing.

WAKE UP AMERICA!

INTRODUCTION

Wake Up! Your life is about to change. You have arrived at a crossroads. You are being offered a rare opportunity. In fact, this is one of those once-in-a-lifetime moments. From this time forward you can begin making choices that will lead you completely, totally, and irrevocably toward financial fitness. Welcome to the road to financial health. There are vast and exciting opportunities waiting for you on this freedom road, and there are challenges as well. For it takes tremendous courage to face the financial realities of your life and choose to stop just existing and start living. In addition to this book, Financial Fitness Centers are located around the country to help you change your life by becoming financially fit.

Most people say that they would like to be debt-free. But those who truly attain financial fitness - those fortunate souls who wake up greeting each new day with joy, excitement, and wonder because they have learned the keys to genuine wealth - these people have decided to stop talking and start walking. They took responsibility. First, with faith in their divine destiny, they made a singular commitment, a contract with themselves. It's a simple contract, but it's one that must be made with the heart and the mind. It's a contract to achieve financial freedom, and it consists of six words, "*I choose to be debt free.*" These words express an all-important first step on an exciting, challenging journey along the road to financial happiness. However, this step in the journey is the hardest, for it requires an act of will. Financial freedom begins with this choice. Only if you are one of those people who are truly ready to learn and apply the principles of financial health should you continue this journey. Right now, ask yourself if you have the courage to "wake up," and regain this vital part of your American heritage - your financial freedom. If you can honestly, loudly, and clearly affirm, "Yes, I choose to be debt free," then you are ready to begin the journey, to discover, accept and use the financial principles that will set you financially free.

Freedom and change go hand in hand. Financial strength and independence can only be achieved one way. You must be prepared to make, and to enact, a number of life-changing decisions. You are going to develop the wisdom needed to successfully live the most important aspects of your life. In exercising this wisdom, you are going to be set free to start turning your most worthy financial dreams into reality. The principles of financial freedom work, but you must practice them diligently, faithfully, and continuously to attain the prosperity and healthy independence you desire. Wishful thinking will get you nowhere. If you desire to advance, you must make these principles a moving part of your life. You must move ahead with your full attention centered on your goal. There are no "quick fix" solutions, no short cuts to success. But if you are truly committed to taking the journey to financial success, the road map you are about to discover will help get you there.

Our American heritage of financial freedom is grounded in the written guidelines provided by the Founders of this great nation. These Founders acknowledged that certain truths are self-evident. Two such truths are that all men are created equal and are endowed by their Creator with certain inalienable rights. That among these rights are life, liberty, and the pursuit of happiness.

To the degree that our nation has honored these truths we have prospered socially, culturally, and financially. By the same token, departure from these truths has led to social, cultural, and financial disaster.

You are about to encounter principles of financial health that spring from these truths. You are about to begin your journey toward financial fitness and freedom. With faith and hope, you are making a commitment to "wake up," and start living, really living, your life.

BUY NOW 2 mi.
HIGH ROAD
PAY LATER 212 mi.
GET RICH
MONEY 5 mi.
ANY ROAD WILL DO
115 mi.
10 mi.
PENNY
CREDIT

CHAPTER ONE

The Road to Financial Freedom

Debt's bondage is no stranger to many Americans. Not having enough money or not knowing how to manage the income we have is a signal that we must take time to learn the basic truths that will lead to fulfillment of our American heritage of freedom from debt. Debt's control of your financial destiny is about to end because you are making the decision to break free from the chains of debt.

As you follow the road map to financial freedom, you will learn several keys to financial health. Like most of life's truths, they are recognized as common sense. By skillfully applying these common-sense principles, you will be able to replace your debt with genuine wealth and financial health.

FINANCIAL FITNESS FACT #1

"It is a good thing that being in debt is not a crime. More people are in debt than aren't."

Financial freedom principle number one: **Budgets don't control your life, they give your life a financial map**. A good budget draws a clear route to your financial health destination. It helps you see your choices and provides you with an opportunity to be aware of and more responsible for the choices you make. A budget opens up your future. It can provide a realistic plan for experiencing the power, the excitement, and the freedom of learning to live within your means. Proper use of a good budget reinforces when, where, and how you will spend your money as you travel the road to financial health.

Financial freedom principle number two: **Getting into debt is easy. But it's easier to get out and stay out of debt than it is to stay in.** It's the "buy-now-and-pay-later" lie that is stealing your dreams and your potential. There is a debt-free day in your future. This freedom principle is going to show you how to reach that day in about one-third of the time you would expect. For example, if you have a home with a thirty-year mortgage, you are going to learn how easy it is to actually pay off that debt in just ten years! You're going to become the holder of a new lease on your own life.

Financial freedom principle number three: **The philosophical difference between being broke and being wealthy is realizing that everyone must either learn how to properly use money or risk losing it.** Understanding the characteristics of accumulating wealth, along with the function of credit, will enable you to systematically eliminate your personal debt.

By accepting and applying these principles and others, you will find that you can achieve financial health and become financially free. You will find yourself "waking up" to personal and communal success. This financial freedom is part of the American heritage you are reclaiming for yourself, your family, and nation.

This is the beginning. In order to know where you need to go, you first need to know exactly where you are. For the next few minutes do the following exercise. It's called "running the numbers." Use the chart on page 5 to list your current *estimated* monthly expenses and to compare them to your present income. It will give you an important first sign post along the financial freedom highway.

If your income exceeds your expenses, great. You might even think this book is not for you, but wait a minute. Do you have a mortgage on a house that you believe you will own someday? If your job suddenly disappeared, would you and your family be financially secure for at least six months, or better yet, a year? Could you pay off all your credit cards right now if you chose to? Do you check the price of an item before you check the quality? If you can answer "Yes" to all of these questions, stop reading. You're already financially free. On the other hand,

RECORD YOUR CURRENT ESTIMATED MONTHLY EXPENSES	
AUTO TRANSPORTATION	
BABY-SITTER CHILD CARE, CHILD SUPPORT	
CONTRIBUTIONS CHARITY	
DINING OUT LUNCH, DINNER, FAST FOOD	
EDUCATION BOOKS, SUBSCRIPTIONS, CLASSES	
FOOD GROCERIES, HOUSEHOLD ITEMS	
GROOMING PERSONAL ITEMS, HAIRCUTS	
HOME RENT/MORTGAGE, IMPROVEMENTS, MAINTENANCE	
INSURANCE LIFE, MEDICAL, HOME OWNERS	
JUST FOR FUN PETTY CASH	
KIDS ALLOWANCES, SPORTS, LESSONS	
LEISURE RECREATION, VACATION, TRAVEL	
MEDICAL DENTAL, PRESCRIPTIONS	
NOT PLANNED "HELP"	
OTHER MISCELLANEOUS	
PAYMENTS DEBT SERVICE	
GIFTS BIRTHDAYS, HOLIDAYS, WEDDINGS	
RECORD KEEPING ADVISORY FEES	
SAVINGS INVESTMENTS	
TAXES	
UTILITIES	
"VICES"	
WARDROBE CLEANING, SHOES, REPAIRS	
EXPENSES BUSINESS (TAX DEDUCTIBLE)	
TOTAL	
MONTHLY TAKE-HOME INCOME	
DIFFERENCE (PLUS OR MINUS)	

if you can't but would like to answer "Yes" to all these questions, then this book can help. If your expenses are more than your income, you're not alone. In fact you are part of the fastest-growing segment of American families. You are in debt, and someone else is in charge of your destiny.

Now let's look at your attitude toward money and purchasing. Take a few minutes to fill in the following "Needs and Wants" chart on page 7. The results might surprise you. Understanding the difference between needs and wants is one of those common-sense guidelines that can put extra money in your pocket almost overnight.

The journey to financial freedom is all about change. It's about becoming financially accountable for your own life, about choosing to live the financial principles that lead to financial freedom. By opening this book you've taken an important step towards financial fitness. You've decided to "wake up" and get your act in shape. Be encouraged. Getting out of debt is much easier than continuing to live in debt. The rewards you'll receive for your efforts are well worth the life-changing commitment you've decided to make.

Wherever you're reading this book, at home, at the office, on your lunch break, at school, on an airliner headed for a business trip, right now it's time to begin rewarding yourself. It's time to stop letting creditors, advertisers, play-now-pay-later-schemers of any kind control your life. These are the choices you must make. You must make them because this is your life, and you've decided to start living it. So

- Choose to learn to live within your means. Don't incur debt beyond your present income.
- Choose to learn to live by your own resources. How long could you and your family survive with zero income? Prepare for your future by planning alternate methods of survival.
- Choose to become informed. Knowledge of how to handle your finances is a major part of achieving and maintaining your financial fitness. Knowledge is a necessary key to freedom.
- Choose to be happy. Regardless of your financial circumstances, the choice to be happy is yours. If money is in

EVALUATING YOUR NEEDS AND WANTS

Evaluate the following list of items by marking "N" for need, "W" for want, and "0" if the item is of no interest to you.

_____Addition to house
_____Arts and crafts
_____Automobile
_____Bicycles
_____Books
_____Bowling league
_____Carpets
_____Cell phone
_____Charitable deductions
_____Children's allowances
_____Checking account
_____China and crystal
_____Christmas decorations
_____Cleaning supplies
_____Clock radio
_____Color TV
_____Contact lenses
_____Cosmetics
_____Dental care
_____Dinner out
_____Education fund
_____Electric appliances
_____Entertaining friends
_____Extension phone
_____FM car radio
_____Food
_____Freezer
_____Fur coat
_____Furniture
_____Garbage disposal
_____Garden supplies
_____Gas, lights, water
_____Gasoline
_____Gifts
_____Guns
_____Hair care/styling
_____Health club
_____House decoration
_____Home repairs
_____Ice cream
_____Investments
_____Jewelry
_____New home
_____Leisure activities
_____Luggage
_____Magazines
_____Musical instruments
_____Microwave oven
_____Medical care
_____New clothes
_____Newspaper
_____Own home
_____Paint house
_____Personal computer
_____Pets
_____Records, tapes, CDs
_____Recreational vehicles
_____Real estate
_____Savings account
_____Second automobile
_____Second TV
_____Sporting equipment
_____Stereo
_____Telephone
_____Tools
_____Toys for children
_____Travel
_____ ____________________
_____ ____________________
_____ ____________________
_____ ____________________
_____ ____________________
_____ ____________________
_____ ____________________
_____ ____________________
_____ ____________________

short supply right now, there are many things you can do that cost nothing but that pay rich dividends. Go on picnics and hikes. Play games with your children or friends. Read together. Happiness is beyond price.

In the following pages you're going to be introduced to many important principles and techniques. A whole new world of opportunities will begin to open to you as you learn them. This is not a passive process. You must become actively involved in the changes that will set you free. You've already begun taking charge by taking part in the first couple of exercises. Let's try another.

Get a piece of paper and write down all of your possessions. Don't leave anything out: your house, car, clothes, even the comb in your pocket or purse. When you've finished, examine the list carefully. How much money have you spent on things that now hold little value? How much of your inventory actually consists of things you have purchased on impulse or without a spending plan? Most people are impulse spenders. That should come as no surprise. Advertisers spend hundreds of millions of dollars each year training people to be impulsive. Imagine the money you'd have if you could follow a plan to resist impulse buying and spend that money on items that will lead to financial health. Picture this - targeting your spending according to a success plan.

The first chance you get, go on a shopping expedition to the nearest mall. This is not a buying expedition. You won't be spending any money, just time. It's actually a lot of fun and very enlightening. Look at everything carefully. Think in terms of long-term needs, rather than immediate wants. You may be surprised at how selective you can become. This will help you to place more value on things you purchase because they will more adequately satisfy present and long-term needs. You might even discover you can actually afford anything you want in that store, but have decided you don't want or need anything. This is the first step in developing an "I spend wisely " attitude. Rather than feeling you are deprived, you'll soon realize that you have been entrusted with a wonderful new responsibility, challenge, and valuable skill. Let's look next at how to develop a plan for wisely managing your money.

TAXES
LEISURE
UTILITIES
JUST FUN
DENTAL
EDUCATION
CHILD CARE
FOOD
DINING OUT
TRANSPORTATION
PAYMENTS
RENT MORTGAGE
MEDICAL
INSURANCE
WARDROBE
MISCELLANEOUS
SAVINGS
INVESTMENTS

CHAPTER TWO

The Fitness Blueprint

If you were asked what's the difference between wealthy, financially secure people, and people who are just getting by or who are in debt, you'd probably answer the rich have money. Well, that's partly true. The well-off also know something else. They know how to properly keep their money. They know the power of wisely constructed *budgets.*

Budget. The very sound of the word is enough to set many people's nerves on edge. It has represented loss of freedom, the end of fun, going without, a life filled with restrictions. Nothing could be further from the truth. Budgeting releases you from the restrictions of debt. People who feel or think they are going without, who lack the freedom to choose when and how they spend what they earn, do so for one simple reason. They are not following a financial plan that will show them the choices needed to enjoy much of the healthy fun that life has to offer. Wise budgeting is the blueprint that will guide your money management choices. It is the spending, saving, and investing blueprint to your financial health and well being.

FINANCIAL FITNESS FACT # 2

"Living your life without the right plan is like building a house with a flawed blueprint. It's destined for failure. Good budgets map the choices that will lead you to financial health and set you free financially."

Many of us are trained from

childhood to spend impulsively. Daily we are bombarded by messages of *plastic happiness*. Buy it now, live for the moment - "freedom" is spelled "irresponsible credit." People who are financially healthy are people who can account for their money. They are people who have learned the difference between plastic promises and real financial health.

The sad fact is that most families live from paycheck to paycheck, with no realistic spending plan, monthly accountability reports, savings plan, or idea of how or when they could be out of debt. In America today the vast majority of families are in extremely poor financial health.

Financial fitness, just like physical fitness, requires a plan of action and the determination and courage to put that plan into action. Developing a budget and exercising the freedom of choice that it gives you is a great part of the foundation upon which your financial health will be built. Good budgets make it possible for you to plan ahead so you'll have cash when you need it. You'll have reserve money along with the attitude and character needed for foreseen *and* unforeseen circumstances. You'll organize your finances in much the same way that successful businesses plan their financial strategies. You'll be making an investment in yourself, your loved ones, and your nation. It's a financial investment that can bring you great joy, happiness, and fulfillment.

You may think that there are too many variables in your life for a budget to really work. But life's variables are one of the most important reasons to build and use a budget. A well-designed budget will help you respond to life's surprises. The more you procrastinate developing a practical, working budget, the more you deny yourself the experience of financial well being that results from carefully planned financial decisions.

So many of us believe that a budget is too confining, that it restricts our financial freedom. In reality, a budget will provide you with the tools you need to realistically plan, accept, and enjoy pursuing your lifetime goals. Knowing how to effectively spend your money and keeping a record of where your money goes is a practice that will assist you in ordering your priorities. Budgeting enables you to make decisions based upon a healthy living philosophy rather than limiting your choices to an unhealthy, impulsive, live-for-the-moment illusion of happiness.

So many people go through life convinced that financial well-being is beyond reach. Part of this resistance to accepting responsibility for personal financial health and fitness comes from false assumptions about budgets. Let's correct some of these misconceptions that keep people from experiencing the joy and wonder of living life within a good budget, free from debt and filled with promise.

- *The only way to really solve financial problems is to get more money.* If you ask a rich person how much money is enough they often say a little more. The fact is, wise budgeting will assist you in finding the solution to your present and future financial goals on existing income.
- *Budgeting is complicated. You need to be a financial expert to make them work.* Budgets are so simple to design that anyone, including a child, can learn to start and maintain one.
- *Keeping track of my money with a budget takes way too much time.* Is 45 seconds a transaction too much time? Once you've got your budget set up that's the average time per purchase it takes to make it work for you.
- *A budget is confining, it restricts my freedom.* This is the biggest lie of all. Budgets do exactly the opposite. They help you spend, save, and invest in ways that can keep you debt free and provide direction leading to greater financial fitness and financial freedom.
- *Knowing where my money went isn't going to help me feel any better.* A budget does more than summarize your spending. It gives you a plan for effective spending. A budget can make clear the vision and goals that motivate you to resist impulsive spending decisions. It gives you the freedom and unique plan to achieve your life's financial goals.
- *If I just take care of my present money crisis, tomorrow will take care of itself.* The present is precisely the time frame a useful budget deals with. Financially healthy people live in a present that is guided by past experiences and directed toward future goals.
- *One of these days, when I have the time, a budget might*

be a good idea. Your financial health is too important to procrastinate about. Budgets are so simple and so effective that waiting just doesn't make any sense. All you've got to lose is insecurity, uncertainty, and unhappiness. It's exhilarating to experience the freedom of personal financial fitness. Wake up and go for it!

Building a budget is much like developing a physical fitness workout plan. Your financial fitness plan depends on your own special needs. Your budget is your financial fitness workout schedule. A fitness trainer uses a series of steps to determine the best plan for your physical development. Similarly, you develop your financial fitness workout plan (your budget) by using the *Financial Fitness Budget Worksheet*. One is included in the back of this book. This worksheet simplifies the creation of a budget. It is an invaluable form that will help you record important information about your financial circumstances. It will lead you through a series of steps that will assist you to manage your income and other financial resources and to track your spending. As you approach this exercise, you will experience a new sense of enthusiasm because it is one of the keys that will lead you to a new lease on your financial life.

A good budget depends on accurate information. Using a budget worksheet allows you to custom design the financial fitness workout that best fits your needs. Knowing your wants and needs is all-important to building a good plan for your budget. Many people are convinced that their finances are out of control. They feel helpless to come up with a system that can help them track where their money goes.

The budget worksheet changes all of that. It illuminates the key information you need to develop a financial fitness plan that will lead to your future fiscal health. This information includes:

- Your income and your expenses
- Your average income and expenses for the previous three months

The worksheet will identify your expenses as fixed, variable, or discretionary. This will help you to adjust your expenses to balance with your income. Part of doing this includes **decid-**

ing which expenses you will pay and when you will pay them. Finally, if you're married, the worksheet will assign responsibility for paying expenses.

The first thing you need to do with your budget worksheet is to create logical and useful budget categories. This begins with *income*. Your most recent tax return is an ideal source for determining your income. Actually, part of the fun of budgeting is using a document that causes so many headaches to help develop a plan that helps relieve you of so many worries.

Once you've determined and listed all your income, you move on to your *expenses*. This usually means doing what's called *best-effort estimating* (unless you're fortunate enough to have developed the habit of saving your receipts as the IRS and tax consultants advise.) Best-effort estimating is a challenge. Start with your bank statements for the previous three months. Divide your canceled checks into the following categories: mortgage payment, auto, contributions, food, dining out, and so forth. This should give you a fairly complete list of all categories where you've spent much of your money during the last three months.

Benjamin Franklin once said,"*'Tis hard for an empty bag to stand upright.*" A special part of creative estimating is the rule of "paying yourself first." Everyone at one time or another feels the desire to spend a certain amount of money without having to explain or justify it. This is personal discretionary money that you are free to spend, give away, or save. The amount decided upon is not as important as the principle. Consider this a personal bonus you award to yourself, to acknowledge your developing financial responsibility and to encourage perseverance with your financial fitness program.

Another special feature of best-effort estimating is planning for the unplanned. On the budget worksheet this is call the HELP category. It is money set aside for unforeseen or unusual circumstances.

In order to begin developing a financially fit physique it is vital to know how you look right *now*! After all, you can't plan where to go without first knowing where you are. The budget worksheet will draw you a financial picture of yourself. This image of where you are right now takes form by estimating your income and your expenses for the last several months. Painting your self-portrait will take courage, but don't back away. The saying "No pain, no gain" has never been more accurate. If you have the courage to follow through with this part of your financial fitness program, the payoff will be tremendous.

Write down the total income you made over the last three months. Now get out your check book and review your canceled checks and bank statement. Separate them into categories that correspond to your budget categories. Next review and list all old bills and receipts. You're looking for anything that could give you information about expenses. Now inventory your possessions to flag recent expenses and spending patterns. Finally, compare your total average income over the last few months with your total average expenses. For most of us, it's not a pretty picture. Facing your present financial physique is like looking in the mirror. But don't give up. In fact, give yourself a pat on the back because you're no longer afraid to look at yourself. You've conquered a fear that keeps so many people from achieving financial fitness. You've begun to wake up!

The next financial fitness exercise in your workout worksheet helps you to take a closer look at your financial physique. Your goal is to bring income and expenses into balance. Some expenses are fixed, some are variable, and others are discretionary. Fixed expenses are monthly payments that cannot be adjusted or changed, for example, rent, mortgage payments, automobile payments, and insurance. Variable expenses fall into a category of monthly expenses whose amounts can vary. You have some control over the amounts. These include items like groceries, utilities, transportation, medical, and so forth. Finally, consider your discretionary expenses. These are items about which you can decide what, or even whether, you will spend *anything*. Examples of these include entertainment, recreation, allowances, contributions, gifts, etc.

Financial fitness includes balancing your income and your expenses. You do this by making adjustments in how and what you spend your money on. You will not be able to make adjustments in fixed expenses because they cannot be reduced. Any adjustments must be made in discretionary or variable expenses because you are responsible for how much you spend in these categories. Making the spending decisions, and more importantly, writing them down, gives you your budget.

Writing down your expenses and income, then balancing them, is the single most important exercise you can do for yourself. If you don't write them down, the exercise won't work for you. If you do, it will. It's that simple. That's what a budget is all about. This budget is your new financial best friend. The decision you have made to bring your income and expenses into balance gives you clear guidelines for spending and managing your resources. It is much easier to follow these spending guidelines than to carry the burden of debt and uncertainty. Where unhappiness and fear have been ruling your life, there can now be confidence and hope. Follow your budget and you will break debt's bondage and find financial freedom.

The next step is to decide how you are going to pay the expenses listed in your budget. Here's how you do that. First list your available income by pay period or on a month-to-month basis. Then assign which expenses will be paid during which pay period. For example, your mortgage payment or rent might be due on the first of each month and would ordinarily be entered into that column for the first pay period. Since this is probably your largest fixed expense, you may need to accumulate income from each pay period until you have the total amount needed to meet this expense. It is important to assign dates, based upon availability of income, when you plan to meet each of your fixed, variable, and discretionary expenses.

Finally, if you're married or share expenses with someone, you must decide who will pay each expense. In some families one spouse may be more interested or competent in this area. In other families the couple may decide to share responsibility. Some budget categories, such as groceries, may be divided between partners, with each being responsible for a portion of the expense.

The budget worksheet is an easy and effective way to paint a financial self-portrait. There are other forms you can use to organize a budget as well. It's not important which ones you use. It's just important that you build your budget using sound and proven principles. The worksheet is the beginning tool of your financial fitness training program. The budget you design provides the guidelines you will follow to develop your financial muscles. It takes determination and guts to start and stick with a physical fitness program. But when you do, the rewards are significant. You look better, you feel better, you're healthier, and you're happier. Once you commit yourself to a financial fitness program, the same dynamics apply. It takes guts, an iron will, and confidence. But the financial freedom that comes with financial fitness is worth the effort.

Some people will say that it is too difficult and limiting to try to live within a budget. Plus, it's no fun. This is a lie. The belief that personal budgets are hard to live with, limiting, and unnecessary is one of the primary factors behind the false promises of the buy-now, pay-later philosophy that Americans are enticed to live by. When you embrace instant consumerism, you pay the price with your freedom and your future. It's far and away harder to live without a budget than it is to live with one.

> *A young man went to an expert counselor for advice on time management. He asked the counselor to help him get ahead in life. The counselor asked him if he was currently keeping up with his duties and responsibilities. The young man answered that not only was he not keeping up, but he was falling behind! The counselor then told the young man that before he could get ahead he first had to learn to keep up.*

The same principle is true with getting ahead financially. Before you can have money to invest in your future, you must first be able to live on your present income. You must first track your spending to see where your money is going. Otherwise you can never expect to get ahead. That's where the *BluePrint Budget Register®* comes into play. It is a special device for tracking spending. It's like having your bank account with you, right at your finger tips, at all times. If you use the sample *BluePrint Budget Register®* that comes with this book for just one month to record your spending habits, you will be astonished at what you discover. More important, you will learn in just thirty days how easy and how much fun it is to keep track of how you spend your hard-earned money.

We are so certain that you will find the *BluePrint Budget Register®* to be an exceptionally valuable tool in aiding the development of your new financial fitness physique that we are offering you this challenge. Use the register for a month. If you don't think it has helped you make better and more effective spending decisions, send us your completed register and we will refund you the price of this book. That's right, use the *BluePrint Budget Register®* faithfully for just thirty days and you will have a new-found ability to make better use of your money. That's our guarantee.

The first page of the *BluePrint Budget Register®* is a suggested CHART OF ACCOUNTS. This is a suggested list of categories arranged alphabetically (it is an easy-to-learn system that corresponds to the categories on the BluePrint computer software available from Financial Fitness Centers everywhere). You can use the chart or feel free to "customize" the accounts to fit your own special needs. If you've made the effort to build a budget using our workout sheet, you can use the categories from that guide instead. You will use a different register each month. Notice the spaces at the bottom of the page for your NAME, the MONTH, and the YEAR to help with recordkeeping.

The remaining pages of the *BluePrint Budget Register®* contain 30 columns. Record the name of each budget category on the top line of each column. Enter a budgeted amount for each category in the $________ space on the top line. You get this information from the budget worksheet. In the months to come you will enter any carryover in this amount, whether positive or negative, in the BALANCE FORWARD space, and this will then be added to the budgeted amount to become the NEW BALANCE.

Each of the budget category columns in the *BluePrint Budget Register®* is a tiny "bank account" where each month you "deposit" the budgeted amount from the budget worksheet. As you begin to spend money from that account, each expense and every expense must be entered into the transaction record as follows:

- **Transaction Type** Enter "C" for cash. Write in the CHECK

NUMBER if you use a check. If you use a credit card, enter the following CREDIT CARD CODE ("MC" for Master Card, "V" for Visa, and so forth).

DATE each transaction.

Description of Transaction Identify each transaction in two ways. On the first line record whom the transaction was paid TO. On the second line record what the money was spent FOR.

Amount and Balance The amount spent for each transaction is entered in the AMOUNT space. This amount is then subtracted from the former balance and a new BALANCE is entered. This becomes your "running balance" of that account. It will allow you to "watch" your spending for that budget category. For example: When a couple of weeks have gone by, if you see the "running balance" in your GROCERIES account is almost all spent, you know you need to curb your spending in that area in order to stay "within budget," or become "overdrawn" on your GROCERIES account.

At the end of one month, you will carry forward any remaining balance in each account - whether positive or negative. This carryover will be factored into the new deposit for each category at the start of each month (subtract if negative, add if positive). This becomes the new amount you have to spend in that budget category during the coming month.

You must carry your *BluePrint Budget Register®* with you at all times. As you make a purchase or spend money, you must record every expense in the appropriate category - **even for a postage stamp or a 25 cent phone call**. Your goal in doing this is to identify where every penny of your money is going! Your confidence will soar once you start using the *BluePrint Budget Register®* to track your spending. Use the register and you will be the one who decides where your money is going. You will be much more able to resist the impulse buying temptation that you often experience when using credit cards. Now you will be able to better plan how you're going to use your money. There's another great benefit to using the *BluePrint Budget Register®*. You can say good-bye to the problem of "evaporating dollars!" You'll know exactly where your money is going. Knowing how you spend your money will tremendously increase your range of financial decisions and capabilities. This knowledge is an important key to your financial freedom.

You're becoming *financially fit*. You'll notice that you have more money in your checking account than ever before, but before you spend it, you allocate it to your budget and your BluePrint categories. The register in your checkbook only tells you how much money you have in the bank. Your *BluePrint Budget Register®* gives you the important information on *how much money you actually have to spend*.

Having an increasing balance in your checkbook can create a lot of temptation to spend budgeted funds for the wrong things. Here's a suggestion that will start you on the way to developing a powerful future financial muscle. Ask your bank to set up suffix or "set-aside" accounts for your budget categories that are accruing balances. A suffix account is a "sub account" within a main savings account that will *draw interest* until you withdraw the money to make periodic budgeted payments (like quarterly taxes, insurance premiums, etc.). Setting up these suffix accounts is the first step toward learning one of the most powerful facts in the financial world. **Those who understand interest collect it – those who don't, pay it!**

If you truly want to achieve total financial fitness, you must record every expenditure in the proper category in your *BluePrint Budget Register®*. You must carry it with you, everywhere you go. You must use it for even the smallest expense. **It must become a must-do habit.** The tracking expenses exercise is like doing push ups and sit ups. It is essential to the development of your future financially fit physique.

We each live a life that is constantly evolving. As your circumstances change, so too must your financial fitness equipment or it is of limited value. Your budget workout sheet, the budget it helps you build, and your *BluePrint Budget Register®* are three tremendously potent pieces of equipment in your personal financial fitness health spa. One of the features that makes them so valuable is their flexibility. Each of them is designed for change.

From time to time, it is useful to complete a monthly budget summary. When you are beginning, doing this once a month is even better. This is like defining or fine tuning your physique. The monthly budget summary will help you evaluate your progress. It allows you to organize your expense record and adjust your spending habits based upon changing circumstances. It renews your budget each month. This builds your budget on a foundation of reality rather than unachievable expectations.

The *BluePrint Budget Register®* gives you all the income and expense information you need to create your new budget each month. Remember, budgets aren't weights to hold you down, they're dynamic tools that help you exercise responsibility over your finances and in so doing help you develop your financial attitudes and financial health. At the end of the first month of using your *BluePrint Budget Register®* do the following :

- List and evaluate all your INCOME categories. Make any changes necessary.
- Do the same with your EXPENSES categories. Add or delete as required. Make the same type of adjustments with budget amounts, pay-period payments, and husband/wife responsibilities.
- Carefully look at any positive balances in your *BluePrint Budget Register®* transactions. You get to decide which of these carry over to the next month in the same category and which are absorbed into other accounts where they can be more effectively used.

  In any given month, unforeseen circumstances will most likely occur that will cause you to be overdrawn in a number of your accounts. The neat thing about this system is *you* decide what you're going to do about it. You might decide to subtract the negative balance from the new month's balance in certain accounts. In those cases, this will give you less funds for the new month, so you'll have to be extra aware of your spending. If you decide that your overdraft is acceptable in some accounts, you can readjust your budget in those areas. Remember, the key is that whatever changes you make, your new budget must start off in balance.
- Look at the discretionary categories on your workout sheet and in your budget. You may have categories that depend

on special money that comes in on an irregular basis. Remember, spending that depends on this type of income can only occur *when the income actually comes in*.

You now have a monthly budget summary. Use this new information to make out your next month's workout plan. These new budget amounts go into your new *BluePrint Budget Register®*

Once you commit yourself to following the financial fitness training steps that have been outlined over the last few pages, you will be well on your way to developing personal financial muscle. Try these exercises for just a month and you'll be surprised how great it feels to begin getting your house in order. Remember that you are making life-changing decisions. "Old" and "bad" money habits are similar to not exercising and overeating; such habits are difficult to change. Forming "new" and "good" money management habits requires desire, planning, and effort. There is no reason to live a life of despair and desperation over money problems. When you start taking responsibility for your actions, you will feel a renewed sense of confidence. Always remember this, **life is the most precious gift on earth**. It is temporary and should not be squandered. Faith, confidence, and hope, together with these financial principles plus hard work, will lead you to a more fulfilling and complete life. It's like "waking up" to a whole new way of living your life – financially fit and financially free. This new way of life could prepare you to achieve one of the most worthwhile financial goals of all. Read on to see how this can happen for you.

LOCAL BANK
0044 2233 0000 9986
JOHN & JANE DOE
VISA

CHAPTER THREE

The Plastic Promise

Do you have a debt problem? Before you answer, consider this. Over 70% of all Americans are burdened with obligations in excess of real income. But is this really a problem? For some people the answer is all too obvious, but what about those of us who are meeting our monthly payments, and maybe even putting a little aside in savings. Let's take a closer look.

Here are some startling numbers. Nationwide, consumer debt, excluding mortgages, more than doubled during the 1980s, to $666.2 billion. In the absence of substantial changes, it is expected to exceed a trillion dollars before the year 2000. In 1988, revolving credit – mainly credit card expenditures – more than tripled, to $185.8 billion. Today it's estimated in excess of $300 billion.

FINANCIAL FITNESS FACT #3

"Those who understand interest collect it, those who don't, pay it!"

In the 1950s (just two generations ago) the majority of Americans made nearly all their purchases, in many cases even their homes, with cash. The two generations of Americans since World War II have grown up with the axiom "buy now, pay later," and the attitude of living beyond one's means has become almost universally acceptable.

A new movement began sweeping across America following World War II. It was the "money revolution." At this time, marketing experts introduced three new ideas that would reshape American society:

(1) The easy payment plan. Low monthly payments made it possible for people to purchase a wondrous array of goods that they only dreamed of in the past. Gradually,

consumers were influenced to shift from saving until they could pay cash to being largely concerned with how much the payments were.

(2) Long-term mortgages. G.I. housing loans were offered to veterans returning from the war. Soon the long-term mortgage became the standard of the home finance market. Mortgages for as long as 30 years became the rule. The American dream of owning a home seemed to become a reality that nearly everyone could achieve. It wasn't long before this fantastic financing freedom was applied to automobile loans. Owning a car, once a goal that required long-term savings became an instant reality with long-term payments.

(3) Credit cards, bank guarantees, and lines of instant credit. Such credit devices became easy to obtain and required no collateral to back them up. It became very easy for consumers to purchase almost anything, and everything. Cash was out, credit was in. The Plastic Society had arrived

Today, proof of the fallacy of this plastic promise is everywhere. Loan defaults, home foreclosures, and bankruptcies occur at record rates. Failed savings and loan institutions and the resulting $500 billion bailout have gravely endangered our country financially. The industrial and retail institutions that earlier benefited from relaxed credit policies are now paying the price in loan defaults that must be passed on to consumers in the form of inflation and higher prices. These are serious warning signs that the time has come for us to deal with the burden of debt in our personal and national life.

Now for the most startling statistic of all. If the current trends continue, according to a 1992 Health and Human Services report, over the next several years only 4 out of every 100 Americans who reach retirement age will have adequate income to live on. ***This means that 96% of us are living a dream that will become a nightmare as we retire.*** **This is your wake-up call America.**

The overuse of easily obtained credit and the general lack of personal savings have placed an unprecedented number of American families at the brink of financial disaster. In the 1980s, it was widely believed that increased consumer spending, regardless of the source of funds, bolstered the economy. We have stretched the maturity dates on loans of all types. Also, because they are one of the few remaining ways to receive tax deductions on interest paid, home equity loans are being used to consolidate consumer debt and this places our homes, the very foundation of our cities and society, in jeopardy. The resulting explosion of mortgage foreclosures has been a major contributor to savings and thrift institutions and bank failures across the country.

Take a look at this list of questions from an organization called "Debtor's Anonymous." Try answering the questions and see if you recognize yourself.

(1) Are your debts making your home life unhappy?
(2) Does the pressure of your debts distract you from your daily work?
(3) Are your debts affecting your reputation?
(4) Do your debts cause you to think less of yourself?
(5) Have you ever given false information in order to obtain credit?
(6) Have you ever made unrealistic promises to your creditors?
(7) Does the pressure of your debts make you careless of the welfare of your family?
(8) Do you ever fear that your employer, family, or friends will learn the extent of your total indebtedness?
(9) When faced with a difficult financial situation, does the prospect of borrowing give you an inordinate feeling of relief?
(10) Does the pressure of your debts cause you to have difficulty in sleeping?
(11) Has the pressure of your debts ever caused you to consider getting drunk?
(12) Have you ever borrowed money without giving adequate consideration to the rate of interest you are required to pay?
(13) Do you usually expect a negative response when you are subject to a credit investigation?
(14) Have you ever developed a strict regimen for paying off your debtors, only to break it under pressure?

(15) Do you justify your debts by telling yourself that you are superior to the "other" people, and when you get your "break," you'll be out of debt overnight?

If you answered "yes" to eight or more of these fifteen questions, the chances are that you have a problem of compulsive debt or are well on your way to having one. The only question left is are you ready to do something about it?

Being in debt is similar to being overweight - it is financial "fat." Before you can be financially healthy, you must eliminate the excess. Whatever the reasons for debt, the effects are often the same as being overweight. Many of the same principles apply for getting out of debt that apply to losing weight. When losing weight, your desire to be thin must be greater than your desire to eat fattening foods. So it is with eliminating debt - your desire to be debt free must be strong enough to overcome the pain of tightening up and sometimes going without.

You have it within you to make changes in your financial life, to get your financial house in order, and to begin establishing and building new habits that will make you financially fit and free. Getting into debt is incredibly easy to do. There is often a feeling of shame in being in debt. The only real shame is not doing something about it. Becoming financially fit is one important way for you to take back your American heritage of freedom. It can and must become the highest financial priority than you can set for yourself. Your future, the future of your children, and the future of your country depend on your following through with the decision you have made to be debt free.

There is reason for hope. Make financial fitness a way of life and you can get out of debt with even greater ease than when you got into it. You can pay off your loans and credit cards, and if it's part of your budget plan, you can own your car and even your home and you don't have to win the lottery to do it. For most people, this is not a question of making more money; rather, it's whether they can wisely budget and spend the income they already have.

There is a "debt-free day" in your future. (How many home mortgage holders really believe they will ever own their home?) Seem too good to be true? Well, it's not. The next few pages could be some of the most important you will ever read. You are about to learn the most powerful financial fitness exercise of all. If you apply these fitness techniques, it will be possible for you to pay off all of your debts, including your home mortgage, in about one-third the time. You can turn your debt into dollars with the Financial Fitness Debt-Free Day Plan, and here's how.

The Financial Fitness Debt-Free Day Plan recognizes a debt as any bill that cannot be paid in cash immediately or will take more than 30 days to pay in full. It begins with a powerful financial fitness tool called the *Financial Fitness Creditor Summary Sheet*. You will find your copy of this powerful form at the end of this book. It is an invaluable form that outlines a series of steps that will allow you to organize and help you implement an effective spending, savings, and investing plan.

When you have completed these steps, you will have an effective plan to become debt free. This will be a key factor in your becoming financially fit and free from financial bondage. Developing an income and expense balance in this important area of your finances will be the basis for building success in many other aspects of your life.

The following is an example of how the creditor summary sheet works. We'll call it the John and Mary Smith sample. It demonstrates how to reach a major part of the goal of financial fitness by achieving freedom from debt. The sample is fictitious, but it demonstrates a procedure that if followed could result in real people, just like you. eliminating debt completely. Using the same procedure, you can turn your debt payments into savings and wise investments.

John and Mary Smith, like many people today, feel a growing sense of concern about their debts. They find loss of future security and happiness represented by their credit card and loan debt, plus the impossibility of ever really paying off their home mortgage, depressing. Like you, they feel it affects every aspect of their lives. They realize that something has to change for their own sake and for the sake of their family. They firmly resolve to do something about it. If they commit themselves to the Financial Fitness Debt-Free Day Plan, they will discover that something truly amazing can happen. Follow along and see. It can happen in the same way for you.

JOHN AND MARY SMITH SAMPLE

John and Mary Smith begin by identifying and listing each of their creditors in the first column on the creditor summary sheet. The creditor with the longest payoff time, their home mortgage, is placed at the top. Each creditor is be added to the list in descending order, with the creditor with the shortest payoff time at the bottom. While doing this exercise, John and Mary remember that a creditor in this plan is someone to whom they owe a debt that cannot be paid off within 30 days. Follow the sample at the back of the book as we go through John and Mary's entries.

The first entry, their home mortgage, is held by the local bank. The current mortgage balance is $58,000 and is being carried at 10.5% interest. The monthly payment is $541 and extends for another 320 months, almost 27 years.

The second creditor is an equity loan on their home at the local savings and loan for $23,000. They want to use the money to add a bedroom and to convert their garage into an office for the health-care products business they plan to run out of their home. The loan is carried at 12% interest, with a payment of $276 for 15 years. This payment, coupled with the first mortgage, brings John and Mary's total home loan payment to $817 a month at fairly high interest.

Assume John's and Mary's third debt is an automobile loan with a current balance of $8,000, financed at 14% interest, with payments of $220 a month for 48 more months. But the car is presently valued at only $6,500, and like many of us, they might question the practicality of their original decision to buy it.

Debt number four is for a major credit card. It has a current balance of $2,100 at 19% interest. The minimum monthly payment is $80. It will take John and Mary 35 months to pay it off – if they make no additional purchases.

Debt number five is a hospital bill. This debt is for $2,500 at 18% interest, or 1.5% per month. The payment is $102 monthly, and will go on for 30 more months.

Debt number six is for another major credit card. It has a current balance of $1,800 and carries 18% interest, with payments of $75 a month that will continue for another 30 months.

Debt number seven is owed to a local finance company.

The balance is $900, again at 21%. The monthly payment is $40, and it will take 29 months to discharge this debt.

Debt number eight is for a gasoline credit card. John and Mary occasionally use it to pay for major car repairs. The balance is $1,600. The interest rate on the card is also 21%. Paying $75 a month, the balance could be retired in 27 months. It would be wise to make no additional purchases with this card.

Debt number nine is for $800 owed to a local department store. John and Mary needed to purchase bedroom furniture. If they borrow the money at 14% interest, they must make 18 months of payments at $50 a month to retire this debt.

Debt number ten is owed to another local department store. Like many people do, John and Mary purchased Christmas presents on time payments and still owe $350 at 18% interest. They need to make $30-a-month payments for 13 more months. It will be Christmas again before this loan is paid.

The last debt on John and Mary's list is for a magazine subscription for $25 that is two months delinquent. They would be charged no interest.

After listing all of their creditors and debts, John and Mary total their current balances and enter the amount <u>$99,075</u> in the DEBT RECAP section of the creditor summary sheet in the box on the first line, opposite TOTAL CURRENT DEBT. They then total their monthly payments and enter the amount <u>$1,514</u> in the box on the second line, opposite TOTAL MONTHLY PAYMENTS in the DEBT RECAP section. They enter the number **320**, which represents the number of months it will take them to discharge their largest debt, their home mortgage, opposite TOTAL NUMBER OF MONTHS TO RETIRE ALL YOUR DEBTS on line five of the DEBT RECAP section. Then they divide **320 by 12 and enter the number 26.6 on line six of the DEBT RECAP section**.

If John and Mary list and total all of their creditors and debts, they can calculate and record their REAL DEBT. This allows them to create a picture of their "true financial bondage." They do this by multiplying the payment for each creditor by the number of remaining payments. When this is done for their home mortgage, John and Mary will discover that their REAL DEBT is not the <u>$58,000</u> current balance, but is actually <u>$173,120</u>.

After John and Mary calculate and record their REAL DEBT for each creditor, they should total these amounts and enter this total in the DEBT RECAP section in the box on line three, opposite YOUR TOTAL REAL DEBT. **By taking these steps, they will discover that their "true financial bondage" isn't the <u>$99,075</u> current debt, but a staggering <u>$245,524.</u>**

Their next step could change their lives forever. They now calculate the interest they must pay to retire these debts by subtracting their TOTAL CURRENT DEBT from their TOTAL REAL DEBT. This interest is a ***whopping*** **<u>$146,449</u>**. They then enter this amount on line four in the DEBT RECAP section, in the box opposite TOTAL INTEREST YOU WILL PAY section.

John and Mary, like all of us, wonder what they could be doing with the interest they are paying to creditors if they could collect it instead. What if they could get it back and invest all or a portion of it? What if they could earn the interest instead of paying it? What opportunities could they take advantage of? What peace of mind could they enjoy? The answer to these questions, and hope for the future, can be found in a tremendously powerful aspect of the financial fitness plan. It is called "debt roll up."

At first John and Mary find it hard to believe that it is possible for them to create a debt-retirement plan that would allow them to **become completely debt free and in about one-third the time that it would take them to pay off their mortgage**. But the more they learn about the *real* power of the debt roll-up plan, the more their skepticism turns to excitement. It really is possible. For it to work, however, they have to practice clear and simple financial fitness exercises. The primary commitment is to add no new debts and to use careful planning and budgeting to control spending.

Then they discover something even more astounding. Using the debt roll up to accelerate their debt retirement *does not mean they need additional income. Nor does it mean they need to increase their payments!* The total monthly amount of <u>$1514</u> they apply toward their debt remains the same.

Let's take a look at John and Mary's creditor summary sheet and see how this can be done. They've recorded their lowest payment on line eleven of the creditor summary sheet. This was the $25 payment for the magazine subscription that was two months delinquent. This bill can be paid in full during month 1 of their plan, freeing $25 that could be "rolled up" to the next creditor during month 2. This payment begins and ends with month 1, and the REAL DEBT is $25.

John and Mary enter the number 1 on line eleven of the BEGINNING MONTH column in the DEBT ROLL UP section. Opposite this, they enter $25 in the PAYMENT column. They enter the number 1 in the ENDING MONTH column, and $25 in the REAL DEBT column.

Next, John and Mary "roll up" the $25 that is available during month 2 to the second department store account on line ten. During the first month they pay the regular $30 payment to the department store; then, beginning with month 2, their payment is $55 [$30 + $25]. They continue making this $55 a month payment until the debt is paid in full during month 8, when they have $42 left over to apply to the first department store debt on line nine. Paying the second department store debt off in full frees the entire $55, which is "rolled up" to the first department store debt during month 9.

John and Mary enter the number 2 on line ten of the BEGINNING MONTH column in the DEBT ROLL UP section. Opposite this, they enter $55 in the PAYMENT column. They then enter the number 8 in the ENDING MONTH column, and $372 in the REAL DEBT column. (The eight-month payoff and the $372 real-debt amount are calculated on a business calculator using the $350 current balance, minus the $30 first-month payment, times the 18% interest, paid out at $55 a month.)

Next, John and Mary "roll up" the $55 that is available during month 9 to the first department store account on line nine. This means during the first seven months they pay the regular $50 payment to the first department store; then during month 8, they pay the regular $50 payment *plus* the $42 left over from the final payment to the second department store. Beginning with month 9, their payment is $105 [$50 + $55]. They continue making this $105 payment until the debt is paid in full during month 13, when they have $93 left over to apply to the credit card #3 debt on line eight. Again, with the first department store debt paid in full, it frees the $105 payment, which is "rolled up" to the credit card #3 debt during month 14.

John and Mary enter the number 9 on line nine of the BEGINNING MONTH column in the DEBT ROLL UP section. Opposite this, they enter $105 in the PAYMENT column. They then enter the number 13 in the ENDING MONTH column, and $873 in the REAL DEBT column. (The thirteen-month payoff and the $873 real-debt amount are calculated on a business calculator using the $800 current balance, minus the $400 paid during the first eight months [eight months x $50 a month], minus the $42 left over from the final payment to the second department store, paid during the eighth month, times the 14% interest, paid out at $105 a month.)

Here are the remaining steps John and Mary will take to reach their **"Financial Fitness debt-free day."** They "roll up" the $105 payment that is available during month 14 to the credit card #3 account on line eight. They pay the $75 payment during the first thirteen months; pay the $93 left over from the final payment to the first department store during month 13; and begin paying $180 [$75 + $105] during month 14. They make their final payment during month 18 and have $30 left over to apply to the next higher debt, the finance company.

John and Mary "roll up" the $180 payment that is available during month 19 to the finance company account on line seven. They pay the $40 payment during the first eighteen months; pay the $30 left over from the final payment to the credit card #3 during month 18; and begin paying $220 [$40 + $180] during month 19. They make their final payment during month 20 and have $68 left over to apply to the next higher debt, credit card #2.

Then John and Mary "roll up" the $220 payment that is available during month 21 to the credit card #2 account on line six. They pay the $75 payment during the first twenty months; pay the $68 left over from the final payment to the finance company during month 20; and begin paying $295 [$75 + $220] during month 21. They make their final payment during month 23 and have $248 left over to apply to the next higher debt, the hospital.

John and Mary "roll up" the $295 payment that is available during month 24 to the hospital account on line five. They pay the $102 payment during the first twenty-three months; pay the $248 left over from the final payment to credit card #2 during month 23; and begin paying $397 [$102 + $295] during month 24. They make their final payment during month 25 and have $289 left over to apply to the next higher debt, the credit card #1.

Next, John and Mary "roll up" the $397 payment that is available during month 26 to the credit card #1 account on line four. They pay the $80 payment during the first twenty-five months; pay the $289 left over from the final payment to the hospital during month 25; and begin paying $477 [$80 + $397] during month 26. This payment is made during month 26 and is their final payment; they have $81 left over to apply to the next highest debt, their automobile loan.

This makes it possible for John and Mary to "roll up" the $477 payment that is available during month 27 to the automobile account on line three. They pay the $220 payment during the first twenty-six months; pay the $81 left over from the final payment to credit card #1 during month 26; and begin paying $697 [$220 + $477] during month 27. They make their final payment during month 33 and have $609 left over to apply to their next higher debt, the equity loan.

Next, John and Mary "roll up" the $697 payment that is available during month 34 to the equity loan account on line two. They pay the $276 payment during the first thirty-three months; pay the $609 left over from the final payment on the automobile loan during month 33; and begin paying $973 [$276 + $697] during month 34. They make their final payment during month 56 and have $84 left over to apply to their last debt, their home mortgage. By paying off their equity loan using the debt roll-up plan, John and Mary cut <u>125 payments</u> from their payoff schedule and saved an amazing <u>$17,000</u> in interest <u>on this debt alone</u>!

With the retirement of all their other debts, John and Mary are now able to apply the entire $1,514, which they had budgeted to pay off their debts, toward their home mortgage. This is a red-letter day for them, one they have anticipated and worked toward. All that remains for them to get completely out of debt in approximately one-third the normal time is to faithfully pay the $1,514 toward their mortgage for the next 46 months. They will not have increased their monthly pay out during the previous five years and can now anticipate being completely out of debt, **their mortgage paid off and their home free-and-clear more than 18 years ahead of schedule.**

They can make their final payment and reach their debt-free day during month 102 and have $102 left over to put into an investment program. After reaching their debt-free day, John and Mary can begin to apply the full $1,514 toward interest-earning investments, fully realizing that **"those who understand interest earn it, those who don't, pay it."** They will have achieved a level of financial freedom that those couples who have not traveled the road to financial freedom can only dream about and will at the same time, have saved an amazing **$92,000** in interest!

Although the **debt roll up** part of the *Financial Fitness debt-free day plan* is extremely powerful and singularly effective, there is one financial fitness exercise that is even stronger! It's called the freedom payment. The "freedom payment" uses the same principle as the debt roll-up plan, but it allows you to accelerate paying off your debts at an even faster rate. The resulting savings in interest makes it worth considering.

John and Mary are shown that any amount of money will accelerate their debt retirement, but if they determine they can budget an additional $200 a month toward their payments, they can get out of debt even faster. Again, in order for the freedom payment plan to be effective, John and Mary must not take on any additional debt, and they must make consistent payments.

Just as they began the debt roll-up plan, John and Mary begin with their smallest debt, the $25 magazine subscription, and pay it off during month 1. They then "roll up" the $25 to the next highest creditor, the second department store.

At the same time, however, they apply their **$200 freedom payment** to the second department store debt, beginning with month 1. Using the same method of calculation they used to calculate their debt roll-up accelerated payment, John and Mary are able to calculate their freedom payment plan payments using adjusted figures that reflect the additional $200 freedom payment they pay each month.

The figures represented in the DEBT ROLL UP + FREEDOM PAYMENT section of the creditor summary sheet *and* in the DEBT ROLL UP + FREEDOM PAYMENT DEBT RECAP section are the result of John and Mary's calculations.

Using this extremely effective method of debt reduction, John and Mary are able to **accelerate their debt retirement and achieve their debt-free day by almost two additional years. In the process, they have saved themselves an additional $10,000 dollars in interest.** Never in all their dreams did they suppose they could get ***completely out of debt in less than seven years.***

Just as this Financial Fitness debt-free day program worked for John and Mary, it could also empower you.

Your prospects of becoming debt free are an exciting reality, regardless of your current circumstances. It is a key factor in your becoming financially fit. To be relieved of the burden of debt, to be freed from bondage to debt, is an exhilarating and empowering state allowing you to take responsibility for your money and financial decisions. Dealing with debt is the core issue affecting almost all other aspects of your life. Getting out of debt is a goal you can achieve and is one of the most worthy goals of your life.

AN OFFER FROM FINANCIAL FITNESS

Fill in the *Financial Fitness Creditor Summary Sheet* that you received with this book. Carefully identify and evaluate each of your debts. While you're doing this, ask yourself why you originally incurred the debt. If you could decide about going into debt for each of these things all over again, would you change your mind? List all your creditors, current balances, interest rates, monthly payments and remaining payments. After you've done this, send us the creditor summary and we will design your personal **Financial Fitness debt-free program** absolutely free. If you do this and make the commitment to follow the plan, you can achieve the ultimate goal of financial fitness and freedom as explained by the John and Mary sample. To learn more about this tremendous opportunity call **1-800-669-8815**.

Oh, one more thing. If John and Mary paid off their creditors in full, the $1,514 monthly payments they had been making could now be invested in their own future. Surprising how quickly things add up. They could cut their creditor payoffs by more than 18 years. *They would then be able to pay themselves $1500 a month x 12 months x 18 years @8% interest for a total of **$720,000.*** **That's what Financial Fitness can do for you. What do you think? Is it worth it?** In the next chapter you will explore your financial philosophy and the powerful roll it plays in your life.

BILL

CHAPTER FOUR

Common Cents

We all have a financial philosophy. We either developed one or fell into one. It's as simple as that. So, what is a financial philosophy? Philosophy is one of those fifty cent words that put a lot of people off. The dictionary defines philosophy as knowledge of general principles or causes and laws - the general rules that furnish an explanation of something. What that adds up to is this. **What you believe about money and how you act on those beliefs, is your personal financial philosophy.**

Whether you choose to accept it or not, you are affected by your financial philosophy. What kind of life you lead, your relationships, your happiness, the things you value, the fundamental person you are, all depend in very large part on the beliefs you hold about money. A study of thousands of financially successful and unsuccessful individuals reveals that what separates them derives more from differences between their personal financial philosophies than from the work they did or the investments they made. A close look at an individual at the end of life will show that his/her success or failure with money was more dependent on personal financial philosophy than any other single factor.

FINANCIAL FITNESS FACT #4

"Wealth is the by-product, not the end result, of a house in order."

It is amazing how much most of us are ready to learn about this singularly important issue in our lives. Personal financial philosophy as a concept is almost never taught in schools and rarely discussed around the dinner table at home. Theoretical textbooks understood by economists and money managers often discuss the subject, but very few books have been written for non-professionals. Many books and magazine articles have been written about the symptoms of financial success or failure, but rarely about the root causes. Generally, there is a lack of understanding about what constitutes a financial philosophy. Your likelihood for success in life will increase dramatically the more you understand your own attitudes toward money that make up your financial philosophy.

A financial philosophy is where success or failure in money matters really comes together. Because of this, learning how to understand and develop your own financial philosophy is one of your most important financial fitness goals. Once you understand the fundamental beliefs you hold about money, you will have at your disposal the potential to become completely financially fit. If you have faith, and the courage to gain and practice the principles of wealth creation, you will achieve the knowledge and lifestyle foundations for a lifetime of financial health

The following quiz, on page 45, examines three widely held views towards wealth. This is not a test for right or wrong answers, but the answers you give do reveal some of your basic beliefs about money. Fill in the blanks with the words you think best describe that attitude. At the same time, circle the statements with which you agree. You may find that your personal financial philosophy is a combination of these prevailing attitudes. Try to pinpoint how you acquired each belief.

Your philosophy about money and wealth, which are symbols for all you own, are the sum total of your experiences and learning. From your very earliest moments, much of your life has been preoccupied with acquiring possessions and property. You have learned many rules affecting ownership, and these rules have influenced your personal financial philosophy. You have had many experiences with bargaining and purchasing or with exchanging one item of value for another.

As your understanding of money and possessions grew, you may have been impressed with the advantage their abundance often gave you, but you may have failed to see the burden of responsibility they brought or how thoroughly they occupied your time and attention. You may have injured someone using the power that money and wealth gave, or you may have been injured by someone using financial advantage in a ruth-

GOLD RULES

(1) More money equals more ______________.

(2) Personal worth is determined by how much ____________ you have.

(3) Everybody knows that _____________ is money.

(4) Everyone has his ____________.

(5) This person's primary focus is on______________.

GOLD CORRUPTS

(1) _____________ is the root of all evil.

(2) It's easier to be humble when you are___________.

(3) Be _____________ with what you have instead of always striving to obtain ___________.

(4) Those who have should freely give to those who _____________.

(5) Make do with what you have or ____ _____________.

GOLDEN RULE

(1) _____________ pays.

(2) Cast your bread _________ ____ _____________.

(3) Everyone has intrinsic _____________.

(4) It's better to teach a man to ________ than to give him a __________.

(5) What goes around _________ _____________.

less or unprincipled manner. This may have altered your thinking about money and possessions, and now you see them as being more harmful than helpful.

Each experience has its affect. This book is intended to provide you the knowledge, understanding, and support you need to regain and maintain your American heritage of freedom from debt.

Most Americans are over their heads in one way or another. Being in debt can result in feelings of shame. For two generations now, our society has been driven by this pursuit of debt. It's so easy to get into debt that today our children are in danger of believing that debt is the American Way. Nothing could be further from the truth. Debt is not healthy for anyone. The debtor philosophy has placed millions of Americans in bondage and stolen their hopes for happiness and security while threatening the very foundations of their personal faith and belief in the American way of life.

- Breaking free from debt's control begins with understanding the primary characteristics of debt. As we said earlier, this knowledge will set you free to begin realizing your dream of financial health. It is how you will regain your American heritage - the promise of life, liberty, and the pursuit of happiness - principles upon which America was founded.
- The debtor is the servant of the lender.

  What is servitude? The dictionary states that servitude is the condition of a slave, the subjection of a person to another person or thing. You may never have thought much about how a financial contract could place you into slavery, but aren't you under the control of anyone who can decide how you spend your income? What happens if you cannot make your payments?
- Giving credit its due.

The Founding Fathers of our nation viewed debt with great concern. The evils of debt were well known, and debt was used only as a last resort in times of dire emergency. But today America has become a debtor nation. How did this happen to the most prosperous nation in the world? It all began with impulse buying, wrong financial attitudes, and the irresponsible use of credit.

In the late 1930s, as a move to stimulate the economy and to try to move the nation out of the Great Depression, the Federal Government took a number of steps in an effort to stimulate the construction industry, which accounts for approximately one-third of the total U.S. economy. A major step was the Federal Housing Administration insurance program, which cleared the way for lending institutions to make what were essentially risk-free loans. These were made with low down payments and extended terms.

Following World War II, veterans returning home from the war were provided with long-term, low-down-payment, guaranteed mortgages to purchase homes. And that has led to where we are today - where virtually all homes are purchased using long-term mortgages.

The mortgage credit system allowed families to obtain

houses while building false and inflated fluid equity. Vast numbers of Americans falsely believe they own their homes. A low down payment, long period for pay back, and tax deduction inducements often lure people into purchasing much more home than they can afford. With such purchases, the accompanying problem of high monthly payments for the mortgage, insurance, and property taxes become big drains on the family budget - all of which are related to the initial value of the house and not the ability of the owner to pay.

Before World War II there were few, if any, long-term mortgages. Typically lenders required a fifty percent down payment and the note was for five years, with a renegotiation at the end of the five years. The prevailing philosophy was that one's home should be free and clear of debt. Families worked toward this goal. Upon achieving it, families often held a mortgage burning party. *Today few people ever envision owning their own home free and clear.*

Consumer credit also began to emerge in America following World War II. Before the 1940s, credit was rarely extended to the general public. Some businesses may have allowed farmers to charge certain necessities until their crops were sold, or some shops extended credit to very select customers, but general credit purchases were very rare. Then oil companies like Texaco and Chevron began experimenting with something new, the credit card, and America's history and heritage began to be rewritten.

Believe it or not, in the 1950s, people saved money to buy cars. Buying a car through a loan was a rarity. Today almost nobody buys a car with cash. The magic of credit, buying something with nothing, has made owning an automobile a part of nearly every American's life. In fact it's so common place we almost consider it one of our rights. But at what cost?

Today, the American economy is almost totally dependent on a constant expansion of credit. But credit is debt. It is spending money that does not exist. Often it means obligating yourself to work longer hours to pay the interest on the money that has been loaned. American industry depends on a continual stream of purchasers. These purchasers often are enticed to buy things they don't need or could get along without. Purchases are made by borrowing someone else's money - credit. Without this credit, industry would sell fewer products, thereby having to cut back on jobs. People out of work would have less money to spend, and the cycle would continue. This is our present state of economic affairs and why we have become so credit-dependent.

Credit leads to long-term debt and this in turn leads to inflation. It goes like this. Long-term debt inflates prices. A 30-year $70,000 loan at 10% interest actually pays off at $221,148. A 21-year $70,000 loan at 10% interest pays off at $167,704. The longer term loan actually inflates the value of the purchase by $53,444. The more quickly you can retire a debt, the less your total investment actually costs you. When purchasing a home, people tend to visualize only the initial cost. Only by looking at the initial cost *plus* the interest can you see the real purchase price. This is true in buying a house, a car or anything where credit plays a factor in the purchase decision.

Bankruptcy is a growing problem that threatens the fabric of all of our economic freedoms. States and municipalities are experiencing increasing financial difficulties. Orange County, previously considered to be one of the wealthiest in California, went into default and bankruptcy in 1994. That same year the inability to repay loans led to over 900,000 individual bankruptcies. Many of them averaged less than $5,000. The cost of these bankruptcies flows to the American consumer in the form of higher prices, frustration and loss of self-respect, and suffering. However, a more lenient financial philosophy often perceives bankruptcy as a way of retiring debt without pain. Some people have filed bankruptcy two or three times without ever correcting poor spending habits.

Sometimes an extraordinary situation will wipe out a person's ability to cope with existing debt. Bankruptcy laws were enacted to mercifully protect people from catastrophes in their lives. In all other circumstances bankruptcy should be avoided at all costs.

- *Making debt-free financial decisions for the long term, rather than the short term, is the primary key to breaking the long-term debt cycle.*

Everyday we hear of ways to become instant millionaires

– sweepstakes schemes, lotteries, gambling, high stocks and mutual funds, ground-floor opportunities. This is called the survivor's mentality, and it's based in false hopes and instant gratification. The truth is that the best way to become financially fit is by making wiser choices *everyday* and never risking everything you've ever worked for.

It's important to avoid developing a survivor's mentality. Learning to postpone consumer expenditures until there is sufficient money saved for them so that no debt is incurred is a discipline that takes commitment and practice. Setting long-term goals that help you avoid long-term debt is also the best form of financial exercise.

The unfortunate term *underclass* has been coined to describe that segment of the population locked in the cycle of poverty. For us, the underclass includes all people who owe money or services. Not withstanding the various reasons, just and unjust, a primary characteristic of this group is too often an adherence to present consumption, which results in present and future debt. Making short-term purchase decisions, living in the moment, and impulse buying are examples of short-term decisions. The principle of delayed gratification will help you avoid falling into the trap of the so-called underclass.

Impulse buying is an example of making short-term decisions. Following a debt-free spending plan is an example of making long-term decisions. A spending plan, such as a budget, consists of many short-term decisions being made daily. But it reflects your long-term goal of being financially fit, by being able to live without going into debt.

Being financially fit involves more than just carefully spending money. It involves individual and family value systems as well as a personal financial philosophy. Individual and family values such as integrity and a good reputation are intangible assets that usually out-value tangible assets.

Tangibles are those things that you can see, feel, and touch. A pot of gold is a tangible. So is a house. Some people have a financial philosophy that leads them to put all their assets into tangibles. Intangibles are typically things which a person cannot see, feel, and touch. Good will, a good reputation, and integrity are all intangibles. These require as much of an investment as do the tangibles, and they earn money much as the tangibles do. People simply value them differently. Over the long haul, intangibles may earn more money than tangibles. The person who says they would rather keep their reputation than a million dollars is wise. The person with a million dollars and no reputation will probably lose his money before he knows it. But the person with a fine reputation and no money will find good ways to earn money or its equivalent.

- *Too often we unnecessarily sacrifice the future for the present.*

  We build gambling palaces even as we let our country's infrastructure deteriorate. We invest huge amounts of money into short-lived entertainment extravagances, while our educational system is on the brink of disaster. Such actions are typical of short-term thinking. They are a reflection of society's interest in "now" consumption rather than in preparation for the future.

- *True happiness and self-esteem are not found in the quantity of things you possess.*

It is a false notion that self-esteem must depend on surplus money. In many financial philosophies success and money are linked together, but often such philosophies are based on appearance rather than substance.

Feeling that you have to "fake it till you make it" is a damaging financial philosophy. In the long run, a home that you can afford will provide you with feelings of more self-worth than struggling to maintain an inflated or false lifestyle. Insisting on having your "dream" home before you can afford it, often becomes a "nightmare."

There are good reasons for owning new and modern equipment, especially if it is in good operating order. But why are we often tempted to trade in an older, functional car for a new one with significantly higher monthly payments and a longer loan term?

Knowingly overspending or purchasing something on credit when you know it will cause a considerable hardship in the future is like scheduling a disaster. Overspending at Christmas time or taking a dream vacation on credit are common examples of scheduled disasters.

- *The interest in credit*

Problems occur when we use credit to satisfy wants instead of needs. The force and power of marketing and advertising on the American consumer are tremendous. Wants overshadow needs. Our financial discipline and self discipline are taxed to the limit day in and day out. Inappropriate use of credit demonstrates our lack of self discipline and can turn instant gratification into a financial nightmare. Commitment to a responsible financial philosophy can protect our dreams from becoming nightmares.

Credit cards and interest go hand in hand. Once you are in credit debt, interest is your companion every minute of the day and night. It never takes a vacation, but it does take everything else. Using credit without going into debt means deciding to buy with great discipline and wise budgeting.

Credit cards are a great convenience and a valuable credit reference - when used prudently. When they are used foolishly, they are like keys to a prison door. The following are good rules to follow when using credit cards: use credit cards only for budgeted items and, most important of all, pay off the entire credit card amount every month before interest payments begins. **Pay no interest!**

Credit is so easy to get and use that we often don't even realize we are abusing it.

Give yourself credit before you use credit. This means think before you act. Here are some examples of credit that you should think about before using.

Many banks offer "overdraft protection." Under certain conditions, such programs can be helpful in protecting you from costly errors. If your bank does not charge an annual service fee for establishing such an account, then sign up for the service. Should you inadvertently overdraw your account, the bank will cover the deficit for a relatively low interest charge. You must go to the bank and pay off the "loan" as soon as you are notified to avoid paying excessive interest charges.

Finance company loans are generally bad economic decisions. In order to receive a loan from most finance companies, you must pledge collateral of greater value than would be necessary to retire the debt. Should you default on the payments, the finance company may seize all the collateralized items. Also, you generally pay a higher rate of interest for money you borrow or for items purchased.

The home equity loan is heavily advertised as a tax advantage loan because the interest you pay can be deducted from your income. This is an obvious advantage over consumer credit, which has no such advantage. However, you must ask yourself if it is worth putting your home at risk just to gain the modest tax advantage. For some necessary affordable and budgeted purchases, such as an automobile, an equity loan may prove better than cash. Interest rates may be lower, and the tax deduction reduces the final, extended amount you pay for the car.

In moments of desperation, desperate people make desperate choices. Pawnshops and "loan sharks" charge very high interest rates and require the pledge or exchange of collateral for their services that may have a far greater value than the amount borrowed. Generally, pawnshops are regulated by state or local ordinances, but their credit policies are rigid, and you may easily lose the property you have left in storage with the store owners if you default. Loan-sharking is also regulated by laws and ordinances to protect unaware consumers from being exploited. But many such "loan sharks" operate outside the law. Dealing with them often can cause you more problems than the circumstance requiring you to seek the loan in the first place.

Borrowing from family members can be potentially dangerous because it can affect good family relationships. It is difficult to keep a family loan "strictly business." It is also difficult to keep a family creditor out of your business.

Never lend more to a family member than you are willing to lose. It is often better to give it as a gift, rather than a loan. Most family members intend to repay as agreed, but when circumstances come up, the money due and the obligation to the family lender may be disregarded. Loaning money to a family member can contribute to weakness. Due to the emotional ties between family members, receiving monetary support can become expected. Those on the receiving end can come to feel "if you really cared about me, you would want to help me."

- *When the money is gone, it's gone.*

As many people go through life, they experience cycles

where they have more money than at other times. When the more affluent part of the cycle is predominant, they often assume that it will continue for some time, and they make long-term commitments based on the current income. If the cycle reverses, the commitments remain but the money to fulfill them may be gone.

When you find yourself falling on lean times, it may be difficult to accept that the current financial situation is *reality*. Continuing to live a life style that is beyond your new circumstances can be disastrous. You may have to take drastic measures to survive. The following suggestions may help you to make the necessary adjustments if you find yourself in this situation:

Avoid false portrayals. Accept the fact that your present financial situation is reality. If the situation is the result of unforeseen circumstances, face it. Live with the present reality, and work for a better future. If the situation arises from poor management, learn from your mistakes, but don't dwell on them or continue to relive them or recriminate yourself. Water under the bridge is water under the bridge. Make every attempt to operate from a truthful and optimistic position.

Avoid all signature loans. Base all collateralized loans on what you would be willing to lose if you had to default.

Don't increase existing credit lines. Sometimes the best defense is a good offense. Work to shrink your lines of credit, rather than to expand them

It's important to keep some of your assets debt free. Safeguard long-term investments, such as retirement programs and life insurance policies. Keep any future inheritances or endowments free and clear.

Do not risk good assets to feed loans. Trying to hang onto a business or an investment that clearly is not going to succeed is a poor decision. Your analysis for ending a business arrangement may tell you that it is not in your best interest to continue. Take decisive action to end it and then move on.

Do not let pride lead you to financial ruin. Continuing to assume an unrealistic life style from your past could be your undoing. Accepting the present situation is always more productive, positive, and ethical.

Developing a working financial philosophy means understanding your own values and setting goals that once achieved will help add meaning and purpose to your life. Life often seems to offer a limited selection of choices. When it comes to money matters, you may find yourself limited to win/lose, lose/win, lose/lose, or win/win situations. It is surprising how many of life's confrontations fall into one or another of these classifications.

WIN/LOSE

In many cases, we find ourselves in win/lose situations. We all grow up in a competitive world. If one team wins, another team loses. In our schools, if our teacher grades on a curve and someone gets and "A," someone else has to get a lower grade. We compete athletically, socially, academically, and physically. As a result, when we enter the adult world of business, it seems perfectly natural to compete on a win/lose basis. Often, we negotiate for the best deal we can without worrying too much about what happens to the person on the other side of the bargaining table. It's called "looking out for number one!"

LOSE/WIN

Life is not a game where there is an absolute loser and an absolute winner. Every arena in life has opportunities for everybody, if approached that way. Everyone can be a winner in some way or another. But, sometimes an attitude of discouragement gets the best of us. We fall into the trap of thinking that if we don't win *all* the marbles we've lost. Also, some of us prefer to let ourselves be taken advantage of rather than disturb a relationship or "make waves." Such people have decided that it's all right to be a loser. In reality, if they would become more involved in the situation, rather than "ducking" the responsibility, they may find that there are ways for everyone to win.

LOSE/LOSE

Lose/lose situations should be avoided at all costs. Imagine two people, like battering rams, standing facing each other and deliberately banging their heads together over and over until one or the other collapses and perhaps dies. The one left standing is the winner, but spends the next year in the hospital in intensive care because of brain damage. In this case, the loser loses, but even the winner loses. This kind of confrontation doesn't make much sense, but it's surprising how often we find ourselves in this kind of situation where nobody can win. It is better to walk away from such confrontations. Why play if you'll both lose?

WIN/WIN

Every situation or confrontation in life has redeeming value. If a person reflects on these possibilities, he usually can find many things to be gained from an experience, even though the primary goal may be out of reach. Relationships that are looked upon and developed as win/win relationships usually last much longer and are more productive than any other situation. There are fewer law suits, fewer divorces, fewer business terminations. In the final analysis, win/win is the only way to go. Life is happier. Life is more positive and less negative. And more opportunities for growth and service are available when we choose to function with a win/win attitude.

Remember the rules that affect how you think about and use money make up your personal financial philosophy. A new philosophy gains power to change old habits once it is written down.

Stop reading this book for a while and think about your desire to be debt free and to be all that you can be as an American. How can the principles we have been discussing help you become a happier person? Would it be worthwhile to develop and live this new philosophy in order to regain your heritage of freedom and freedom from debt? The answers to questions like this are the foundations upon which a healthy financial philosophy is built. This process has already begun if you have tried some of the exercises described earlier in this book, especially if you have taken the time to fill out a budget worksheet and have experimented with the enclosed *BluePrint Budget Register*®. Invest some time to identify objectives for your financial future by doing the following :

- Write your *one-month* goals regarding planning and budgeting.
- Write your *one-month* goals regarding getting out of debt.
- Write your *one-year* goals regarding accumulating more

money and possessions.

- Write your *one-year* goals regarding planning and budgeting.
- Write your *one-year* goals regarding getting out of debt.

Your personal financial philosophy is made up of those rules that affect how you think about and use money. And the key is, the rules that affect how you think about and use money are nothing more or less than your written goals for the next month and for the next year. If these goals reflect a healthy and wise financial philosophy, then you will be on the way to freedom from debt and genuine financial health. These goals can be your rules and become your financial philosophy. A goal that is not written down is only a fantasy. A goal that is not pursued is only wishful thinking. If you will write down your goals and pursue them, your newly stated personal financial philosophy can become a source of great inspiration and satisfaction. It can become the framework for the development and achievement of true financial fitness and the freedom to really live life that comes with it.

Review your monthly goals (rules) every month. Promise yourself that you will faithfully do this. Then keep your promise. Write down your review date on your calendar for each month for the next entire year. Make it a habit.

Review your annual goals (rules) on a special day each year. Write down your review date on your calendar. Make it a special event like your birthday because reviewing and upgrading your financial philosophy, goals (rules), attitudes, and beliefs is like a fresh start. You might even consider giving this special event a special name, something personal and meaningful to you, something that gives it the attention and the importance it demands.

Enter into an agreement with someone you trust and to whom you can be accountable regarding your goals (rules). Being addicted to a poor financial philosophy can be like being addicted to alcohol or drugs. Breaking away from this addiction can be difficult. You may need help. There is help available, and it's more fun and usually better to have support.

Remember that you are making life-changing decisions. An old and bad money philosophy is difficult to change. A new money philosophy means developing new habits that take desire, good planning, and consistent effort. You *are* your philosophy, whether or not you are aware of it. So choose goals (rules) that will change your attitude toward money and possessions, and that will reflect a financially fit philosophy. **Wake up and start living it!**

The next chapter will help you to give your children a head start in developing financially fit attitudes. It's never too early to "wake up" to the benefits of achieving financial freedom.

USE OUR
LAYAWAY
PLAN
YOU
GOTTA
HAVE 'EM!
Which Blue Is You?
ZCAVARICCI LEVIS
GIRBAUDS GUESS
DOCKERS mixed
BLUES
SALE
GUESS
?
JEANS
APPAREL
DO IT.

CHAPTER FIVE

Children and Money

To some they are the Pepsi Generation. Others know them as Generation X. But, what today's children and teens really are is the *Credit Generation!* Shopping has become our national pastime. The fastest growing area of spending is *by* and *for* the almost 50 million children aged four to twelve years – a figure that is drawing near the $100 billion mark annually! In addition to this, 30 million teenagers pump almost $250 billion into the economy each year. This ready, impressionable, and growing market has made today's generation of young Americans the obvious prime targets for every sales device and strategy that powerful marketing and advertising strategists can dream up.

There is a battle being waged for the financial hearts and minds of our children. It is a struggle with a billion-dollar payoff. The media-driven onslaught aimed at children to buy the "hottest" and "latest" is causing fundamental changes in our society. The need to be "in," to "measure up," to own the right clothes, toys, school supplies, cosmetics, and more has never seemed more important to children.

FINANCIAL FITNESS FACT #5

"Attitudes and beliefs about money, its use and abuse, begin at home. Our children's future happiness is mortgaged and stolen from them when we fail to provide them with a firm understanding of the reality of finances."

Money is easy. It's never

been easier to get or to spend. This is a most significant piece of misinformation that our children are receiving as they grow up. Recently, many large banking operations announced plans to provide credit cards to children beginning at age twelve. In addition children will soon have access to their very own ATM cards.

In America, children and youth generally have the greatest amount of unencumbered, disposable income, plus they are the most influential controlling factor in a majority of family purchases. Children represent one of the most powerful groups of consumers today. What they learn early in life about responsible consumption, credit management, and personal accountability can make or break their future. Unfortunately, today's care-free children will become tomorrow's young adult financial failures. This is a national tragedy, but fortunately it is one that we can do something about.

The children in your family need strong and reliable support as they confront all the strategies that marketing and advertising use to influence their attitudes towards spending and, ultimately, their future financial abilities and decisions. Your spending habits, your attitudes towards the use and abuse of credit and toward money in general will determine the future success and happiness of your child. This is why it is tremendously important that you start early in teaching your children how to understand and manage money. Children must have accurate information about credit, interest, and all other areas of financial responsibility. Remember, wisdom and knowledge are keys to financial freedom. The younger children are when they start to learn healthy fiscal exercises, the more financially fit and free they will be as adults.

AS THE TWIG IS BENT ...

A tree farmer renowned for growing a special variety of trees, one with long, straight-grained wood that grew remarkably straight and tall, invited a journalist from a national magazine to visit his farm. The journalist knew the farmer sold his trees and lumber all over the country and that a human interest story on how the farmer raised his special trees would be popular with his readers. But, as the journalist ap-

proached the tree farm, he noticed something very strange. A strong wind was blowing across the adjoining farms, and it was clear it blew almost constantly because all the trees in the hedge rows and windbreaks looked to be permanently bent. When the journalist arrived at the tree farm, however, he noticed immediately that all its trees were growing straight and tall, in spite of the wind. When he met the farmer, he asked him about this. "Yes," said the farmer. "There is a prevailing wind that blows through here most of the time."

"Then how are you able to raise such straight trees?" the journalist asked.

"We give them strong and reliable support to help them stand straight against the wind," said the farmer.

The journalist looked at the trees and scratched his head. Then he said, "And that's all you have to do?"

"Yes," said the Farmer. "That's all we have to do. But the real key is that we start when they are very, very young."

SO GROWS THE TREE...

The success of any program designed to help children and youth learn the importance of good money management lies in beginning early. The rewards will lie in knowing how to budget, how to avoid debt, and how to properly manage credit. Children and youth must be well founded in these skills in order to avoid the lure of easy-money advocates. A child's success will be influenced by a clear understanding of how to properly make money grow. As we approach the challenging prospects of teaching these principles to young people, it is vital to have a clear understanding of where the family - both children and parents - stand right now.

Share this **Youth Money-Management Questionnaire** with your children. It focuses you on money-management issues that may not have concerned you in the past. Answers should be marked "T" for true or "F" for false. This is the beginning of a series of good financial fitness exercises that you can do with your children. So don't be judgmental or critical. Don't lecture or suggest changes at this point. Listen carefully to their reasons, evaluate what they have to say, and include their views into your family's financial fitness program.

T F (1) Becoming rich is not one of my main goals; there are more important things to do than make money.

T F (2) I think a lot about what I could do to make money, or more money, now and in the future.

T F (3) I earn most of my own spending money.

T F (4) I can account for all the money I earned and spent last month.

T F (5) I have a plan for saving money, and I save a certain amount each month.

T F (6) In the past I saved more money than I do now.

T F (7) When I get old enough to drive a car, I would buy a new car on credit rather than wait while I save enough money to pay cash for it.

T F (8) If someone sent me a pre-approved credit card, I would use it without giving any consideration to the interest I was being charged when I used it.

T F (9) I prefer to ask my parents for money as I need it rather than get by on an allowance for which I have total management responsibility.

T F (10) My parents frequently say "no" when I ask for money to buy personal items.

T F (11) I know approximately how much my family spends on me personally each month.

T F (12) My parents "owe" me more than just shelter, food, clothing, and medical care.

T F (13) I believe it is important to be completely honest in all of my financial dealings with others, even though there are times when I could realize personal gain with a little deception.

T F (14) I have made some plans for my future and even tried to imagine where I will be in 5, 10, 20, 40, or even 60 years from now.

This questionnaire is a revealing look at your child's attitudes about money and money management. It gives you and your children an opportunity to discuss feelings about wealth, jobs, earnings, savings, credit, allowances, honesty with money, and financial planning. Children will believe that financial fitness is important if it is an obvious vital part of the family structure.

What is the source of your child's attitudes about these important money management concerns? Do they derive from inside or outside your family, or both? What plans do you presently have for providing training to your children and answering questions about money management?

Now answer the following Parent Money-Management Questionnaire. It is designed much like the youth questionnaire. The same principles apply. The purpose of the questions is to provoke thought about certain attitudes and behaviors. The questions relate to two specific areas of financial concern: your children's money and your children's possessions

T F (1) I consistently give in to my child's demands for more things, whether I think he or she has earned them or not.

Some parents feel that it is important always to reward their children monetarily when they perform household tasks or duties. On the other hand, some parents feel that these rewards can become nothing but bribes, when every request to perform a household duty is met with "How much will you pay me to do it?" How do you feel about how you are teaching your child about the importance of earning money and things?

T F (2) I give my child a regular allowance and allow him or her to decide how to budget and spend it.

Some parents feel that managing an allowance gives a child an early opportunity to learn about such things as fixed, variable, and discretionary spending. At the same time, other parents feel that receiving an unearned allowance gives a child a false sense of the value of money. Making decisions about a child's finances can be complex and personal. How are you teaching your child to handle money and to make decisions about its use?

T F (3) My child's room is filled almost to overflowing with toys and other fun things, largely because my neighbor's children have the same.

Does your attitude about your child's possessions reflect your attitude about your own personal possessions? Is it important for you to "keep up with the Jones's?" Which are you more interested in, satisfying the needs or satisfying the wants of your child? How are you teaching him or her about the differences between needs and wants?

T F (4) I periodically require my child to inventory and evaluate his or her possessions to determine their present practicality and usefulness.

This question asks you and your child to address attitudes about the usefulness of possessions. Some parents feel that a child's possessions are only a means to an end, and their present usefulness to the child reflects their true value. Other parents feel that all possessions are an end in themselves and have an inherent usefulness, whether or not they or their child is presently using them. How do you feel about your own personal possessions? Is this attitude consistent with your demonstrated attitude toward your child's possessions?

Let's take stock of the toys your children have and how and why they got them. Once again, this exercise does not judge right or wrong; it simply shines a very revealing light on your attitudes, and by example, your child's attitudes on the value of money and possessions

In most homes, there is a box filled to overflowing with toys and other fun things. In storage there often is another box, this one filled with unused or outgrown toys. Other toys and recreational equipment lie idle in the garage or scattered about the yard.

(1) Assemble all of the toys from the toy box, all those from storage, and all those lying about the house or yard.

(2) Using the special *Financial Fitness Centers Toy Inventory Sheet* at the back of this book, complete an inventory of each item by first recording its name, brand, cost, and current condition.

(3) Evaluate each item as to its current recreational or educational usefulness. Estimate the amount of time your children have played with it or used it.

(4) Note which items your children received as gifts, such as for birthdays or for Christmas.

(5) Note which of the items your children worked to pay for, or paid for with their own money.

(6) List which items were purchased to fill a child's new interest in a project or hobby? Did the child follow through to completion or did he or she lose interest and abandon a partially finished project?

To value something means that we hold it in high esteem or prize it as something of worth. The value of something is a reflection of its desirability, usefulness, or worth. People usually value that which satisfies their needs and wants, generally that which brings them pleasure, approval, and acceptance rather than pain, disapproval, and rejection.

Shaping children's values, specifically "what they consider valuable," is the primary objective of a never-ending million-dollar marketing and advertising campaign. Modern electronic media techniques are tremendously effective in shaping children's decisions about values. Your challenge as parents is to arm your children with a **sense of true values** so that they will be able to freely make decisions about what is and what is not really important and necessary to enjoy a healthy life style.

The following six suggestions have been found to be effective exercises in teaching children the value of money as it relates to satisfying needs and wants.

(1) **It is never too early to teach children that money is payment for labor performed.** When parents pro-

vide money without teaching this principle, children tend to become consumers rather than producers. As they consume, it is not readily apparent to them that all goods and services are secured by the labor and effort of someone. Parental indulgence can deprive children of the opportunity to learn these basic elements of financial responsibility. They are denied the opportunity to consent to and contribute to the well-being of the family. The logical consequence of receiving without effort leads children to expect reward without expending effort.

(2) **Children need to be taught that work is not only the way to meet daily needs but is also the way to develop resourcefulness, personal responsibility, and a sense of confidence and worth.** Often, adults who are deprived opportunities to perform meaningful work find that their self-esteem suffers greatly. Your child's work ethic is influenced by his contact with you and other role models. If you demonstrate enthusiasm and creativity in your work and talk about the positive benefits of work, you child is likely to adopt similar attitudes. However, if you regard work as an unfair burden and as mere drudgery, your child will likely look at it the same way.

(3) **In order to communicate the positive aspects of money to children during their most impressionable years, they must be introduced to it at a very young age.** Many parents have been successful introducing it to children as soon as they are able to count, through such devices as play money, real coins, games that utilize money, home-made checking accounts, savings plans, etc.

(4) **"Those who understand interest, collect it; those who don't, pay it."** This concept is one of the most important you can teach your children. Learning early the value of earning interest gives your child a tremendous advantage in developing and securing their future financial fitness and the freedom to enjoy life that comes with it. Teach them to calculate interest. Emphasize the value of having a good credit rating now, at home, and in the future.

(5) **Children need to learn how to plan spending in advance.** Some parents have found it valuable to involve their children in planning menus and shopping for the needed items. Some have shown them how to estimate the cost of the meals beforehand, how to use shopping lists, and how to use savings coupons. Parents have also found it valuable to educate their children about the value of quality and about unit pricing and sizing and so forth. Effective planning and spending should be taught at an early age. Remember : "As the twig is bent . . ."

(6) **Finally, it is vitally important that children learn at the earliest age how to make wise spending decisions.** Healthy interdependence, independence, and personal responsibility are developed by making choices, right choices for debt-free living. Children need to be taught that when making spending choices with money, the money is gone and a better choice is no longer possible. This will help them to learn to plan ahead before making money decisions. If your children do not learn to make good choices while under your supervision as a parent, they might never learn the downside of poor money management.

The most meaningful spending decisions for children are made if they are using their own money. A child must not dictate how a parent's money will be spent. A parent may decide upon the amount of money that can be budgeted for new shoes. If the child wants shoes that cost more, then he or she should be allowed to pay the difference. Ideally, this difference should be earned before the purchase is made. A child should not be allowed to purchase the shoes before they earn the difference. If the money is advanced by the parents to purchase the shoes interest should be charged on the advance that is made to them (as a general rule children should not be allowed to borrow from parents or to pay interest.) Such teaching opportunities can be used to show that in the adult world of money management, it costs to use someone else's money. A corollary to this is that children should not be allowed to dictate a lifestyle beyond the income level of the parents.

It is said, **"If we fail to plan, we plan to fail."** By not helping our young people to plan and prepare for the complex and challenging times ahead, we doom them to failure. As a parent you must teach your children the principles of effective money management. The Financial Fitness Centers have developed a fun and effective program for systematically teaching the skills and habits that will help young children learn how to manage money. This financial planner for children is called *Mr. Money*. In much the same way as you are learning to develop your own personal financial plan, Mr. Money will help your children to do the same thing. Mr. Money helps children to identify and write down goals. It encourages children to plan their saving and spending, before they actually save or spend their money. The Mr. Money financial planner shows children how to work towards goals, how to be responsible for their own income, how to keep records, how to evaluate how they feel about money, and how to handle it.

> As a bonus for investing in your future by buying this book. The *Mr. Money Financial Planner For Children* is yours, free! Turn to the back of this book to get the simple details on how to receive this fun and valuable financial fitness tool for your children.

One way to show love for your children is to *not always "bail them out"* when they get into financial difficulty. Teaching them how to avoid financial predicaments is a better way. Teaching them about planned spending, consistent saving, financial responsibility, and goal-setting for the future could be called "success insurance," which may be the best insurance of all.

One of the best ways to start your children on the path to financial responsibility is to teach them to dream. Dreaming is a powerful motivator. Dreams are a vital part of your family's financial fitness program. Without dreams, it would be difficult to have goals that can truly motivate you to new levels of financial awareness and mastery. Actually, it is almost impossible not to dream. As you imagine and dream about how things might be if you and your family were debt free, these processes become a vital part of your decision-making, your direction, and your future. People who have healthy financial principles can discipline themselves to become debt free if they wish to. Wise and healthy values can result in realistic dreams that can provide the necessary motivation for your children to develop financially fit practices that will guide them to financial freedom as children and as adults. It is one of the most valuable gifts you can give them.

Listening to your children's dreams is very important. Helping them to cultivate those dreams according to wise financial principles and helping them work in accordance with these principles in healthy ways will forge a bond of trust between parent and child that can last a lifetime.

Complete the Youth Money-Management Questionnaire and Parent Money-Management Questionnaire. Use them as a basis for determining where you and your children stand right now regarding your attitudes about money and possessions. This will prepare you to move ahead in helping your children to learn the basics of a good money-management system that will get them started in the right direction down their own road to financial freedom.

Introduce your children to their own Mr. Money financial planner. Assist them with writing down their goals, making financial plans, keeping records, and looking over their month's-end review and evaluation. Your efforts to help them become good friends with Mr. Money and his financial planner will give them a road map for their financial futures.

Remember, you are helping your children to make life-changing decisions. As they learn to use these new money-management tools, their skills will grow, and they truly will become like highly trained athletes on the playing field of life, financially fit, free, and the beneficiaries of their American heritage.

As a final exercise, sit down and review the following two charts with your children. They graphically demonstrate the value of saving and of collecting interest. Learning the exciting truth of these concepts early on gives them a tremendous jump start on their future.

THE POWER OF COMPOUND INTEREST

The following chart demonstrates how a small savings deposit of $10 per month will increase with time at various interest rates.

Interest Rate / YEARS	5%	7%	10%	12%
10	$1,553	$1,730	$2,048	$2,300
20	$4,110	$5,209	$7,594	$9,893
30	$8,323	$12,200	$22,605	$34.950
40	$15,260	$25,248	$63,240	$117,648
50	$26,686	$54,480	$273,244	$390,583

This next chart demonstrates how a one-time investment of $1,000 will grow with time at various interest rates.

Interest Rate / YEARS	5%	7%	10%	12%
10	$1,755	$2,105	$2,753	$3,281
20	$2,984	$4,280	$7,300	$10,366
30	$4,986	$7,612	$17,450	$29,960
40	$8,248	$14,974	$45,260	$93,050
50	$13,560	$29,457	$227,390	$389,002

WHAT IS THE RULE OF 72?

The Rule of 72 describes how compound interest works. If you divide the number 72 by the interest rate you are receiving, the result is the number of years it will take your investment to double.

For Example: If you are receiving 6% interest, divide that into the number 72, which equals 12. This means that it will take 12 years for your investment to double.

Financial fitness is closely tied to your total well-being. Let's look next at how financial fitness can help reduce the stress you feel in daily life.

CHAPTER SIX

Stressing Out

Imagine the following scenario. You walk to your mail box. When you see the contents, you begin to feel ill. With mounting anxiety you notice several envelopes with windows and company return addresses. Your bank statement is there and a card telling you that you have a registered letter at the Post Office. As you return to your house, you can feel your stress level rise, and as you open your bank statement you completely lose control – there are several charges for overdrawn checks. Your need for money is greater than ever, and the penalties for your overdrafts have consumed the little bit of money you thought you had in your account.

FINANCIAL FITNESS FACT # 6

"Financial problems lead to stressful lives. The resulting desperation is not living, it is merely existing. Financial fitness and freedom means understanding the specific role out-of-control finances play in creating stress and learning what you can do to minimize financially stressful situations."

If you could take a look inside your body, you'd discover that the medulla of your adrenal gland was pouring its adrenaline into your blood stream in excessive amounts. Adrenaline generates many physiological changes. Under stress, adrenaline influences the liver to release stored sugar into the blood stream. Chemical changes occur that cause your blood to clot more quickly. Your blood pressure rises, your pulse beats more rapidly. The air passages into your lungs enlarge to admit more air. The pupils of your eyes enlarge to gather more light. Sweat breaks out all over your body, particularly on the inner surfaces of your hands. The temperature of your skin may rise or fall several degrees. Your body is in stress mode.

Stress mode provides a temporary energy boost, but it taxes the body and requires recovery time. If the conditions persist that caused the pressure, the individual will suffer permanent damage.

Stress is epidemic among Americans today. In the business world we see intense competition, layoffs, mergers and acquisitions - all taking their toll in derailed careers, broken families, and emotional problems. More and more people are affected by the stressful and unfulfilling aspects of modern life. Work obligations and family obligations, rather than supporting one another, are in direct competition with each other, which leads to increased stress. The signs are everywhere. Increased drinking and drug abuse, family and spousal abuse, and the resulting tragedy of familial breakdown.

The modern American lifestyle that stresses quantity over quality is filled with stress. This is a major contributor to business loss as well as individual and family breakdown. Studies show that the cost to business of stress-related problems and mental illness is estimated at $150 billion annually in health insurance and disability claims, lost productivity, and other expenses

Adding to the stress level is the fact that while each day nearly five thousand Americans turn 65 years of age, only four out of every one hundred of these people have substantial financial assets to allow them to enjoy a secure retirement. More than 60 percent of retired people are living on less than $10,000 per year. The majority of them have no individual retirement funds. The reality of shifting gears at age 65 from productivity and financial stability to unemployment and Social Security income can be extremely stressful.

A significant contributor to individual stress is the lack of financial security. The feelings of threat and hopelessness that result when a person sees his assets disappearing because of debt, or even worse, because he realizes he has no assets at all, are perhaps the most notable cause of stress today. On the other hand, stress can be seen as positive because it motivates a person to realistically appraise his or her financial condition and begin making the necessary commitment to the total lifestyle changes prerequisite to becoming financially fit and financially free.

A financially healthy company does everything it can to protect its assets. A healthy company is marked by three important characteristics: mobility, stability, and credibility. When these three characteristics are present, the company is able to pay its stockholders dividends, maintain and upgrade facilities, fund research and development, and provide valuable incentive programs to increase work productivity. When any of these characteristics are lacking in a company, it is said to be in stress mode. Stress mode often results in down-scaling. It cuts incentive programs for employees, puts research and development on the back burner, and neglects routine maintenance of facilities. If this condition persists, the company can crumble and fold under the weight of debt.

Just as financial stability is essential to industry, it is also vital to individuals and families. In order to achieve freedom from financial stress, individuals and families must work hard and wisely to care for their assets. Possessing adequate resources to meet all your financial commitments and needs means that you have a financial philosophy and plan that emphasizes mobility, stability, and credibility. When you incur debt that you can not reasonably pay, when the funds on hand are not enough to meet expected needs or possible unexpected emergencies, your financial life loses these characteristics, and you are headed into *financial stress mode*. And, there's an even greater asset than money that you need to value and protect. This great asset is your spirituality. It is from our spiritual source that we gain the energy that provides us with the means and power to accomplish everything in our life that is worthwhile - all our work activities, our creations, and our relationships.

Individuals and families, faced with the reality of stressful day-to-day challenges, need to have a positive foundation in five major areas: *spiritual, mental, emotional, volitional, and physical*. When we learn how to utilize the positive aspects of these areas, we will be happy, healthy, productive, and stable human beings; and we will have learned to minimize the negative influence of stress.

Self awareness is a first step to success in any endeavor. This is especially true when confronting the effect that stress has on the quality of life. The key to minimizing the stress in your life is to learn and use accurate and specific information. There are many effective stress management programs. All of them should enable you to identify specific causes for your stress and present potential corrective actions that might help you minimize the negative effects of stress on your finances and, therefore, on your life.

The following present examples of real-life concerns that for many of us lead to stress reactions that can negatively affect every aspect of our lives. The examples may or may not apply to your situation in every case. However, they are a good guide for determining stress self knowledge and for effectively recognizing the role financial concerns and good financial planning has in managing stress in all aspects of our lives.

FORM-A-PHOBIA!

Almost everyone is faced at some time or another with the need to fill out forms, such as financial statements, loan applications, job applications, state and Federal tax returns, and more. Each time we fill in forms asking for information about ourselves, we are confronted with the condition of our personal finances. Because of the lack of a thoughtful financial philosophy and a realistically applied personal financial plan, this is more often than not a very stress-filled activity. For some people, just thinking about forms increases their stress level. The key to dealing with this type of stress is planning and preparation. First, a well designed and effectively applied budget such as we have discussed in this book removes nearly all of the stress from this activity. Second, easy access to information (something as simple as a shoe box filled with receipts, insurance policies, etc.) goes a long ways towards managing the stress in financial self-evaluation that forms require. Additionally, having a daily planner where you keep a record of your on-going expenses, transactions, appointments, dates, etc., is tremendously valuable as a stress reducer. Always keep in mind the results you are trying to achieve when faced with the task of filling out forms. Remember that penalties, late fees, increased interest, loss of credit rating, and other lost opportunities are all examples of what can happen when you feel overwhelmed by lack of information and planning.

THE MORE GENUINE SELF-CONFIDENCE YOU HAVE, THE LESS STRESSFUL LIFE IS

If you have developed a high degree of confidence, you tend to get more enjoyment out of life's challenges. There are many paths to increased confidence, but there's nothing like the experience of healthy success, especially in your financial affairs, to raise your confidence level. This means learning to take the time to evaluate your actions and decisions, weighing the possible liabilities and gains of your financial choices. It means being willing to learn, to expand your personal "bank of knowledge" in all areas of your financial life. This can include attending classes or seminars on effective ways to manage money, reading books on financial and personal growth, and gaining advice from financial experts and consultants. Part of developing confidence means accepting responsibility for your own actions. Your bank statement is yours. It is up to you to balance it, to keep records of your deposits and your debits. Even if your situation calls for the services of a personal bookkeeper and accountant, in the end you are responsible for your own financial decisions. Remember, experience is a teacher. Learn by studying and doing. Making mistakes is part of this process. Not repeating the same mistakes is the goal.

FACE IT, YOU CAN'T ESCAPE IT!

"Getting away" seems to be the goal all too often when facing financial stress. When your income is much less than your living expenses, when reminder notices make up most of your mail, when all avenues to improvement seem to vanish, it seems natural to want to just get away, escape somewhere, let it all go. The trouble is, life continues, decisions are made, financial obligations are still in force, and of course, interest never sleeps. Stress grows commensurately with the degree to which we put off facing responsibilities.

Stress is reduced by taking wise action. This includes facing all your financial challenges no matter how large or overwhelming they seem. It is possible to do this when you have a good inner balance based upon exploration and understanding of the true purpose of your life. When you can achieve inner peace, it becomes possible to confront life's problems with confidence and hope. This includes returning calls from creditors even if you do not have the means to make payments at the moment. When you do not communicate with those to whom you are financially obligated, the situation can quickly get out of hand and becomes more drastic and stressful. Try writing down the major sources of your stress in your life and what you can do to possibly eliminate them. These solutions may not be perfect, but they are a step in the right direction. Although many factors may have influenced you or contributed to your present financial condition, only you can choose to change it - to begin learning to manage the life decisions that lead to stress. As you start to exercise this choice, you will be amazed how it develops your confidence, how other people will begin to honor your decisions, and how much stress is relieved by confronting unpleasant situations with positive energy and actions. Depend on your faith, take the first step, use your new knowledge, and the rest will come more naturally.

CHOOSING TO DO WHAT MUST BE DONE

It is normal for all of us to resist doing what must be done occasionally. But sometimes these feelings must be set aside and replaced by action. If your spending is exceeding your income, choose to temporarily down-scale your standard of living. Choose to seek ways to increase your income and to better manage what you are currently earning. By choosing to do these things, you eliminate the stress caused by feeling compelled. As soon as you choose to do something rather than doing it because you feel compelled, the negative demand for energy in your body caused by related stress diminishes, and creative energy increases.

Try focusing on getting tasks done one step at a time. Set time limits for completion. When tasks drag on, they tend to become high-stress activities. Again, it is a good practice to use daily planners and to set down goals guided in part by reasonably designed budgets. Short-term goals are just as important as long-term objectives. It is important all along the way to have measurable successes of your efforts to achieve financial freedom and independence. If you tell yourself you're going to do it, do it. Keep self promises. Keep promises and commitments to others. Start with little things. Small achievements lead to future successes. Soon you will find negative demands and stress being replaced by positive energy and the sense of freedom that comes from making wise choices and keeping your word to yourself and others.

KEEPING TRACK MEANS STAYING ON TRACK

People who keep accurate records and who insist that things be kept in proper order are seldom in financial difficulty. What if an airline advertised, "Sometimes we arrive safely?" By consciously choosing to keep records, to do things on a reasonable schedule, you can prevent the emotional stress of last-moment decisions. It takes much more time and energy to do things over than to do them right the first time. If record keeping is difficult for you, ask yourself why. Does it seem unnecessary? Is it because writing materials are never handy? Do you tend to lose the notes you make or misplace the receipts you've managed to keep? *It is difficult to get ahead if your are barely keeping up.* Learning to set aside time in which to do tasks is an important key to stress reduction. By scheduling blocks of time into your daily activities (a great use for your daily planner), you will be able to get more things accomplished. Keep a record of your day. It only takes a moment to jot things down, and the payoff can be tremendous. An information center is vital to your accurate record keeping. Rather than having slips of paper scattered all over, keep them in one place.

SHOPPING FOR STRESS

Some people love to shop. Some even consider it to be a form of recreational therapy. Others hate to shop and avoid it whenever possible. But all of us do shop. The different ways that people shop can make a big difference in their finances and the resulting stress. There is a big difference between shopping and buying. Shopping is searching for, pricing, estimating, wondering, trying on for size, and so on. Buying is parting with hard-earned money. Both unmanaged shopping and impulse buying can lead to increases in stress.

A wise shopper is guided more by needs than by wants. Shopping is done as part of an overall financial plan. Avoid purchasing items that are unnecessary and unwanted. Shop for particular items. Avoid browsing, wandering aimlessly down aisles looking at everything. Shop with a purpose and a goal in mind. Impulse buying, even at sales, is never part of an effective financial fitness plan. Just because an item is on sale doesn't make it a good buy. Buying something just because it is on sale can lead to overdrawn checking accounts or blow your budget. Always try to consider the cost-per-use of the things you buy. Something that will be used only once or twice is evaluated differently than something that will be used constantly.

Buy quality. A good pair of shoes that lasts may cost a little more but will result in savings over the long run. Discipline yourself to buy only when you can afford to buy. Let your budget be your guide. Try saving ahead for things you desire. Be more willing to down-scale when necessary. Guard against complaining when you can't have just what you want when you want it. Follow this maxim at all times: unless it fits, unless it works, unless it is necessary now, do not buy it.

Do not become a prisoner of your possessions. You cannot purchase happiness or contentment. These are qualities that come from within and are based upon a belief in a higher purpose for life than just being a consumer. This is so important to remember. You are not your possessions, your purpose in life is not guided by what or how much you own but rather by what and who your are. Contrary to the popular slogan, the winner at the end of life is not the person with the most toys. Life is not a game or a contest, but a gift, part of a continuous evolving miracle. You cannot shop for or buy inner peace. This comes from living a life filled with purpose according to the spiritual values and beliefs that guide you. Discovering your purpose and how to achieve it is one of the primary reasons for pursuing financial fitness and financial freedom.

DON'T DELAY, LIVE TODAY

Self starters are in the minority. Yet when things need doing it is best to take responsibility and do them correctly. This is a good way to manage the stress that comes from feeling a lack of responsibility for your own life. To delay means to put on hold, and you cannot put your life on hold. The longer you wait to make a commitment to a task, the greater the stress exerted in your life will be. Whenever you procrastinate about a needed task, building a budget, getting in shape, starting a savings account, paying a bill, etc., ask yourself the following, "If not now, when? If not me, who?" When you delay life's decisions, you negatively affect yourself and your loved ones. This in turn jeopardizes your opportunities for success. Every action produces a reaction. Inaction simply produces reverse results. For instance, if you choose to avoid paying bills, you automatically choose to accept the penalties and resulting stress that accompany not paying them. If you choose to justify your actions (or inaction), you may find that only you are convinced by your arguments, and that your family and friendships suffer as a result. Each time you fail to perform, you are encouraging what is simply a bad habit. Each time you fail to perform, your self-confidence and your ability to change is weakened. Each time you fail to perform, you increase the stress in your life. The resulting disappointment, irritation, or anger only contribute further to the stress that may be threatening your life.

LIFE IS CHANGE. IT'S FACING AND MAKING DECISIONS

Everything that happens is preceded by a decision. There are four primary alternatives to every decision: take action, delay, let someone else decide, ignore the situation entirely. Each alternative is a *decision*, whether you want to admit it to yourself or not. If you avoid making a decision, you are actually making one, the results of which you may not be able to control. Once you understand that you cannot avoid making some kind of choice, you will discover it is easier to take action than to delay or defer.

Making wise decisions and implementing them is a key to success. Relying on your life-changing decision, in spite of opposition, may be the key to effectively eliminating stress in your life. Where there is a will, there is a way. Learning and applying new financial concepts can be exciting. Most decisions are guided by emotions rather than by careful consideration. This fact is well known by marketing and advertising experts. Learning to rein in your emotions when it comes to your financial affairs is an important step both in gaining financial independence and reducing the effect of stress on your life. When you are faced with major choices that affect spending and resources, try to project the long-term effects of the choice. Unless it is an emergency, take at least 24 hours before making a change that is of any significance.

STRESSING STATUS

The amount of money a person has does not necessarily determine his or her freedom. We frequently hear of millionaires who go broke. Having money does not mean having freedom. At times it can even produce the exact opposite. You can be more successful at living your life than some millionaires, and your status, your self acceptance can be much more personally satisfying. Each person is unique. It is important to develop your own particular talents and abilities. Often when we treat others with fairness and as equals, our own need for the approval and recognition of others seems less important. As we become content in knowing that all people have value, our own stress from rejection becomes less frustrating.

It is important to learn sound business principles as part of our overall personal development.

To be truly free does not depend on the size of your bank account. It does depend, however, on the bank account being well managed. Learning and applying good living habits in all areas of your life is an important way to reduce life's stress. Be constantly prepared to learn the lessons that life is always teaching. Avoid the temptation to appear to be something that you are not. Always, "to thine own self be true ..." and you won't be untrue to anybody else. This is central to financial well-being and personal happiness.

SECURITY OVER STRESS

Security may be defined as the freedom from danger, risk, care, poverty, and stress. We all spend our lives seeking security.

Many times we believe that security will come with a good job, a higher income, a better living standard. However, life is risk. If someone else takes the risk, someone else makes the profits. When the day comes that your employer cannot make a profit from your services, you will find that your security is threatened. But the reality is that true security must come from within. External security is only an illusion. So too, your financial security, in the final analysis, is a result of choosing to live according to healthy values and wise financial principles.

Most people work for someone else, and they prefer it this way. They are filling a vitally important role in our country and our economy. By constantly upgrading your skills, you will better insure your usefulness and longevity on your job.

Many people are becoming increasingly successful in home-based businesses or other income-producing activities outside their primary employment. After you secure your basic needs, you can pursue other means to augment your income.

Current economic trends suggest that it will become increasing difficult to live on Social Security at retirement. It is difficult, yet very important, to secure future financial security. Begin now to find something that you love doing and that can help you now to provide for your future needs. Many firms offer retirement plans, but it is better to depend on your own abilities and talents. This is especially true if you find yourself moving from firm to firm. Begin making independent plans for your retirement, as early as possible.

Good financial planning is key to security. Accelerated mortgage and other forms of debt liquidation can save thousands of dollars and years of payments. Saving is a habit that must be learned and once learned can lead to a lifetime of security and freedom from stress. Wisely investing even small sums on a regular basis can yield high returns. Always be open to investment opportunities but never invest more than you can afford to lose.

Stress affects the quality of all of our lives. Financial problems and concerns are a major contributor to the stress each of us must deal with to one degree or another. Arguments over money are a leading cause of many family breakdowns and the increasing rate of divorce. It is impossible to over emphasize the importance of taking responsibility for your finances in the battle against stress. Learning how to live by sound and usable financial principles can tremendously reduce the amount of stress in a person's life. It is not a question of more money at any cost but rather one of recognizing bad financial habits and practices and replacing them with newly learned good ones. Stress disappears as we become more responsible for our own lives. Our confidence in our ability to live a secure and fulfilled life grows as we move towards financial security that comes with the application of sound, personal financial practices.

A vital part of financial freedom is learning to recognize the things we have and to be grateful for them. Stress is a by product of living a self-destructive and unfulfilled lifestyle. It is one result of a society that has become consumed by consumerism. The race to own more and more material things at the expense of developing a healthy life based upon experiences, spiritual guidance, and a sense of wonder and appreciation for life itself results not in obtaining happiness but in increasing stress, and a lack of purpose or understanding of what life is all about. Living a life that is in balance and free from stress means accepting financial responsibility. It means developing a driving desire to learn and contribute. It means accepting that meaning and purpose exist beyond mere possessions. Financial freedom is not achieved in a vacuum. It comes from making life-changing, and stress-reducing choices in all aspects of our lives - spiritually, mentally, emotionally, volitionally, and physically.

Properly reducing the stress in your life can free you to improve those things about yourself that can make you valuable and successful. In the next chapter you will learn about methods for doing just that.

CHAPTER SEVEN

The Successful Advantage

You are your most important product. Financial success is a part of your "self" product. If you want to succeed, you must first have a game plan, a plan that will enhance your productivity and increase your ability to handle money and other resources wisely. You need to establish goals and go after them. To be successful you can and must learn how to play to succeed.

Productivity and success work together to help you down the road to financial freedom. They depend on each other. Productivity without a sense of accomplishment and contribution loses its sense of meaning. At the same time, success will never be fully realized unless it is the result of working a plan that leads to a sense of accomplishment. *Notice how these two concepts are tied together.* They have many things in common, but the three things they have most in common are wise values, planning, and work.

FINANCIAL FITNESS FACT #7

"That which will ultimately make you succeed or fail is already within you."

True success comes only from productivity and a sense of accomplishment, wise personal values, and contribution. Almost everything of value that you have in your life comes as a result of your productivity. Sometimes people are born with monetary advantages, or benefit from unexpected windfalls or rewards over which they have little control, but these are not the stuff successful lives are made of.

Productivity is how much you are able to accomplish. It has to do with filling the needs you have based on what is important to your life's purpose. Your productivity is influenced by your values and your goals. It is also influenced by your current inventory of needs and your plans for reaching your goals and filling your needs. *Productivity is making things happen - especially those things that fulfill your destiny as designed by your Creator. This is also called success.* Usually, you achieve this kind of success because you have a plan, you have faith, and you let them work together.

Who's in charge? That's mostly what success is all about: who's in charge of your life? Today in America, as we face the challenge of learning how to manage our financial affairs, we are faced with two important choices: Will I be content to allow others to control what happens to me and my finances? Or am I willing to do what is necessary to become responsible for my financial affairs? This is what success is all about. Who's in charge. It is a matter of will and choices and whose will and choices are directing your life, in the right pathways.

Undoubtedly, there have been happy times in your life when you felt that you were making financial decisions that were consistent with your spiritual values and life's purpose. Everything seemed to be going right. You felt genuinely successful at accomplishing what you had set out to achieve. But at other times you may have felt less successful. You may have felt that you were being pressured and pushed around by forces you couldn't control. Maybe you wanted to blame the bank or the landlord or your parents or your boss. Maybe you wanted to blame "city hall." But whomever you blamed, you felt that somehow you were not in charge of things, and you blamed everybody but yourself for your lack of success.

As you think about it, what was the difference between the times you felt successful and the times you didn't? Probably it had to do with whether or not you felt you were making decisions that were best for your health, decisions that were true to your relationship with your Creator and others. Even when you felt that you were in control, you may have experienced that temporary, but false, sense that you were totally in charge and no challenge seemed too great nor any problem too difficult. Then when you realized that other, often impersonal, forces were pushing you to and fro, you lost your clarity of purpose and your ability to purchase only what was really needed and found yourself increasingly discouraged. This was when going into debt and feeling that you were losing the ability to live out your destiny set in.

When discouragement takes over, we seem to lose energy and interest in doing productive things. We often feel lost and hopeless. We also feel worthless. Sometimes overcoming these feelings of hopelessness and worthlessness isn't easy. Usually it's because we don't know how to change. We may have forgotten that success begins with an act of *will*. Will I be content to allow others to control what happens to me and my finances? Or will I do what is necessary to choose the principles of finance that will lead to financial freedom? The following, "Jane's Story," is an account that describes how using financial freedom principles and talents can increase your income.

JANE'S STORY

Jane lived in a big rambling house out in the suburbs. The only problem with the house was that it seemed like she had to spend too much time cleaning it and cleaning up after her husband Bill and her children. So she decided to figure out ways to have the family work together in cleaning more efficiently. This made her work go faster and easier. Eventually she became an expert at house cleaning. She could clean her house in almost no time at all, and as her ability to manage and do house cleaning increased, Jane found herself experiencing joy in her work. Soon her reputation among her friends and neighbors as a good house cleaner grew to awesome proportions.

Then one day Jane and Bill decided that the family needed some extra money. To fill this need, Jane got a part-time job working as a clerk in a convenience store earning a minimum wage and working for a boss that was a grouch. From that time on, Jane's life was the pits! She hated her job and her house was always a mess, even though Bill tried to help. Somehow, taking the part-time job did not seem like such a good idea, and the money just wasn't worth it.

Seeing Jane's unhappiness with her job, Bill very tactfully suggested that maybe she needed to re-think what she was doing. Maybe she should look for some other kind of part-time job. Maybe she should go with her strengths and try doing something she enjoyed.

Jane looked to herself and took stock. She asked herself three very important questions: What are the most important values I have in life? What kind of work do I like to do best? What kind of work do I actually do best? By asking herself these questions, Jane immediately realized that the answer had been there all the time, staring her in the face! Her family was most important to her. She liked house cleaning best, and she was good at it!

She talked it over with her husband and family and then Jane asked her friends and neighbors if any of them needed occasional "expert" house cleaning. Some of them did and said they would be excited to have Jane do it because they knew how good she was. She asked them if they had friends who might want house cleaning done, and of course they did. Jane's circle of prospective customers was growing. She and Bill formed a licensed, bonded house cleaning company called "Jane's Expert House-Cleaning Service" and started doing business. Soon she had so much work she had to hire and train helpers to use her effective cleaning methods. Eventually, she incorporated, and Bill quit his job to help her manage the business. Now, she is able to oversee the cleaning efforts of her workers in the houses of her customers, making sure that everything is just right! She focused on her skills and went with her strengths. We believe that this story illustrates principles that have resulted in many happy customers for Jane and Bill.

When Jane first tried to earn money to improve her family's way of life, she failed to consider one of the most important rules in productivity and success: you are your most important product.

The point of this story is that you have the interest and resources to build a life toward financial freedom. All you need to do to begin is *wake up* to your very own special talents, abilities, and skills that will enhance your productivity and success. Part of waking up your financial strength means taking stock of yourself. Asking and answering the following seven common-sense questions will help you do exactly that:

(1) What kind of work do you do best?
(2) What kind of work do you like best?
(3) What is your most obvious talent?
(4) What other talents, abilities, and skills do you possess?
(5) What can you do to enlarge your talents and to improve your abilities and skills?
(6) What income-producing tasks can you think of where you can use your talents and skills?
(7) Who can you talk to for advice on how to enhance your income by using your strengths?

Your productivity and success are like your own special team. They depend on each of the many and varied aspects of your personality and character to succeed. They depend on your strengths. In order to have a successful "productivity team," you must clearly identify your special strengths that help to make you what you are. You must write them down. Then you must think about and plan how you can use them to help you achieve a fulfilled life. You will be better able to recognize your weaknesses and use them together with your strengths to maximize your potential for success. You will be developing a growing relationship with your Creator, self, family, friends, and nation, and be in a position to experience financial freedom and health.

As your financial fitness grows and you wake up to a developing sense of financial freedom, you may find that you have talents, abilities, and skills that you have forgotten. Ask yourself the following questions designed to stimulate your thinking about the unique talents and abilities of your own successful "productivity team":

- Every vocational activity focuses primarily on people, data, or things. Is your natural focus on people, data, or things? What is your secondary focus?
- Are you more comfortable working indoors or outdoors?
- Are you more comfortable seated or standing?
- How do you balance your need to seek greater opportunity with your need to be secure?
- Are you more comfortable working with the creativity and theory of an idea, or with the application?
- Is your work rhythm slow or fast?

- How concerned are you with the details of a job? With workmanship?
- Do you enjoy competition in your work?
- Which do you prefer, working for commission or salary?
- Do you consider yourself to be a self-starter?
- Do you enjoy traveling in your work?
- Is your focus physical or mental?

People who take responsibility for their finances are people who have a plan that is based on correct financial principles. They plan ahead for needed cash. They reserve money for foreseen and unforeseen circumstances. They organize their finances in much the same way that businesses plan their financial strategies. But the sad reality is that many people who feel they are out of control with their finances (and with personal development) either have no plan or the wrong plan. They live their lives without a clear road map or destination in mind, not knowing where they are right now and not knowing where they are going.

Imagine a large ship in the middle of the ocean with a captain who has not properly charted his course. It's a big ocean, and the only landmarks are the ocean currents and the sun and moon and stars. Imagine being on an airplane with a pilot who has no idea of where he is headed. He looks out the cockpit window and sees mountains and streams and lakes and an occasional community. He sees roadways crisscrossing the terrain below him, but he has no idea where any of the roads are heading. He is lost. He has little chance of getting you where you want to go, and on time!

If you are to be successful in enhancing your productivity and increasing your income, you must clearly define (1) what you need, (2) whether if those perceived needs are consistent with your life's purpose and destiny, and (3) whether this plan is guided by understanding and acceptance of healthy spiritual values.

Let's take a closer look at Jane's story. When Jane and Bill made the decision that Jane would take on a part-time job, it was not immediately clear to them what they would gain from her efforts. At first, they were just looking for some extra money. Soon, however, they found that Jane's life's priorities, family, happiness, and peace of mind, were more important. When Jane left home to work as a clerk in the convenience store, she no longer had time to keep the house as clean and orderly as before. Bill was willing to adjust his schedule to help her, but the routines he'd developed in his life and the press of his own busy work schedule were always in conflict. Jane suddenly found much of her time being regulated and controlled by her new boss, someone she often disagreed with, someone she came to regard as a "grouch."

Later, when Jane and Bill decided to start the house cleaning business, Jane discovered satisfaction in doing a job she was good at. She also felt a new sense of personal worth as she made what she considered to be an important contribution to the lives of her customers, her friends and neighbors. She realized that these good feelings were things she wanted very much, maybe even more than the money.

As things turned out, Jane and Bill made a lot more money in the house cleaning business than they had ever imagined they would when they made the decision for Jane to work outside the home. Their entire lives changed in ways they had never expected once they clearly defined what it was they needed and developed a plan to get it.

Your financial freedom will largely be determined by how often your choices are guided by belief in, and acceptance of, healthy spiritual principles. If your financial goals are in conflict with other goals in your life, you can never feel completely free. *A financially free and healthy individual pursues a fully integrated lifestyle.* ***This means developing and applying a living philosophy that is spiritual, mental, emotional, volitional, and physical.***

You must try to discern what level of financial independence and freedom in your work is necessary for you. Unless and until you are able to do this, you will always feel a sense of dissatisfaction with what you are doing: Too little freedom, and you will feel controlled and manipulated; too much freedom, and you will feel lost and helpless.

You must be willing to correct your course when you veer off the road. You must be willing to learn from your efforts, not just your mistakes. This is called *product enhancement. You*

are your most important product, and you must be willing to change things about yourself and what you are doing.

You must be willing to raise your expectations and deal with the challenges and opportunities made available by your own success. Productivity will always bring new fruits into your life: new skills, new friends, new ways to use your time, new opportunities, and sometimes new problems. Through increased productivity, you will "wake up" a new found sense of financial strength. This may allow you to go farther and get there faster than you ever thought possible.

"Waking up" your financial strength means choosing financial principles to live by that are firmly based in an understanding and acceptance of sound spiritual values as well as healthy physical and mental disciplines. You can not achieve your maximum financial development unless you commit yourself to reviewing and improving your total life through the application of health, spiritual, mental, emotional, volitional, and physical practices. A healthy body-, mind-, and spirit-based philosophy is needed to determine where you're going and how you're going to get there.

- **Goals must be written down.** Goals that are not written down will rarely be more than dreams or wishes. Writing down a goal makes it real.
- **Goals must be your own.** If you borrow a goal from someone else, the true power of commitment will be lacking from your plan. Without commitment you'll have little or no chance for success. (Completing the questioning process detailed below will help you assure that a goal is your own.)
- **Goals must have real benefits.** A goal must be able to answer the question: "What's in it for me and others?" Real benefits mean real value, positive change, or improvement.
- **Goals must allow you to change.** A goal must allow you to reach out, to stretch and grow. A goal must allow for positive movement. A goal must also be flexible. Working toward a goal will always change you. As this happens, you may need to make some adjustments in the goal itself.

- **Goals must contain a completion date.** If your goal doesn't have an arrival time, you'll never know for sure when you've arrived, or if you've arrived. Without a completion date you really don't have a goal.

Every good plan must effectively answer the questions what, why, how, when, where, and who. The answers to these questions will give you the basis for your strategies for success and the boundaries of the field of play.

(1) **What** is your top priority, your most immediate goal? This choice is especially important: enhanced productivity and increased income will be a result.

(2) **Why** do you want to achieve this goal? Write your reason in a single sentence. This sentence must describe why this is your top priority in enhancing your productivity and increasing your income. If you can't state your reason or reasons why this goal is most important in a single sentence, you won't be sufficiently focused to make your most successful run at it.

(3) **How** will you achieve your goal? What is the first thing you will do? What is the second, and so forth? Make a list. Make a step-by-step plan. Make a flow chart. Just as you would plan a cross-country trip, plan how you will achieve your goal, one step at a time.

(4) **When** will you achieve your goal? Set time tables for each step along the way. Set completion or arrival dates.

(5) **Where** will you have to go, each step along the way, as you work toward your goal? Almost every journey toward a goal takes you some place physically, to a new place of employment, to a materials supplier, to a potential buyer for something you have produced, to school, to a seminar, to an opportunity meeting. Almost every journey has interim physical destinations along the way. You need to clearly write down where these destinations are.

(6) **Who** will you get to know as you work toward your goal? Some of these people will be vital to the successful achievement of your goal. (Some of these people may not even be living people: for instance, your goal may include studying historical records to get to know successful people who are no longer living, or you may deal

with animals who take on the role of personalities as you work with them toward your goal.) Who of these people will you contact in person? Who will you contact by phone or letter? These people may be customers, teachers, students, counselors, mentors, fellow workers, advisors such as lawyers and accountants - or any other persons with whom you will associate as you work toward your goal. Often it's how much you know, together with whom you know. One thing you can always count on is that nothing much ever happens until two people come together to effect an exchange or bargain.

(7) Are these goals consistent with your life's purpose and of benefit to you and others?

When you are satisfied that you know the answers to these questions and your plan is firmly in place, you will be well on your way to achieving your goal.

Your productivity and success depend on many different aspects of your makeup: your skills, your personality, and your mental and physical posture, including the way other people see you and are affected by you. Working to succeed demands special attention to and training of your total personality

A good point can be made that every individual who has the opportunity to read and study this book has more than enough innate talent and ability to make himself or herself financially free - to succeed! But some of them will succeed while others will fail. Why is this? The answer is simple: *People who succeed plan wisely and act consistently. People who fail, fail to plan and then act foolishly.*

Three basic strategies for success are the broad, narrow, and creative strategies. Each strategy has its advantages and disadvantages. As you consider these strategies, you may discover that in most cases, successfully playing the game will include all three strategies. Each has its place in your success planning.

When you use the broad strategy, you try to cover as much ground as possible as quickly as possible. This allows you to get the broadest sampling of ideas, opinion, information and, ultimately, opportunity! An example of the broad approach would be to send out a hundred or more resumes, hoping that one or two will result in an appointment, interview, or opportunity. Another example of the broad approach would be to advertise or promote your product or service through a mass-mail approach, hoping for a one- or two-percent return from those people showing some degree of interest. The primary disadvantage of the broad approach is that generally you cover a lot of territory with limited results. Much of the ground you cover is infertile.

When you use the narrow strategy, you focus your attention on a very select target market for your idea, product, or service. The advantage of the narrow approach is that it allows you to concentrate a great deal of effort toward making a particular contact work for you. An example of the narrow approach would be to select a particular business, research the business to learn all you can about it, and then write your proposal or design your resume specifically to fulfill the expectations and exclusive needs of this business. The primary disadvantage of the narrow approach is that it can leave you with all your eggs in one basket.

When you use the creative approach, you create a job or new opportunity for yourself. You may approach a particular firm but create a new way to fill a need for the firm that is not presently being filled. Or you may establish a business for yourself. An advantage of the creative approach is that you are free to use your talents, abilities, and skills. You are less dependent on the participation and limitations of others. Often this approach showcases your greatest strengths. An example of the creative approach would be to propose to a business that you will work for them without charge for a period of time, with the intent that you may find some unfulfilled need and be able to suggest profitable ways to fill that need - all with the ultimate end of creating a job for yourself with that business. Another example of the creative approach would be to invent a new device or solve a product or service problem and promote and market this new idea to customers or clients. The primary disadvantage of the creative approach is that you are always covering new and untried ground. It's possible to head up blind roads that don't lead you to your goal. It's also possible to make mistakes that slow your progress toward your goal.

Productivity and success have their own special rules. Those who succeed have become experts in these rules. The following is a list of those rules that are most important:

- The "me" rule states: I am endowed by the Creator with my life's destiny and all the potential to achieve it.
- The "you" rule states: The more I know about others I relate with, the better chance I have of serving and succeeding.
- The "24-hour" rule states: Everybody in life has the same 24 hours in which to work.
- The "focus" rule states: Each step is taken one at a time
- The "right tool" rule states: Each part of my body is a specialist.

It doesn't make much sense not to live to succeed. Yet, that's what many of us do. We live like those who plan to fail and so we live unfulfilled and often in debt. We may lack confidence. We may not think we're good enough. We open our eyes in the morning and think about the day feeling depressed. Maybe we think that the secret to the success of others is that they have some special advantages and have more hours in the day to practice and get the job done. Maybe we're not focused, and our plan is disorganized. Maybe we don't know our own strengths well enough and are uncertain whether or not we are good enough to compete. Just showing up isn't good enough. If you expect to succeed, you must plan, practice, and live according to wise life principles based on sound moral values.

Remember, the "me" rule states: I am endowed by the Creator. You are your most important product where productivity is concerned. Accept yourself for what you are, but use what you are to build, choose, plan, and act wisely. When you use the "me" rule, everything you do will result in two important things: improvement in yourself and in your self image.

You are unique. Your talents, abilities, and skills, all have special value. Your productivity and success is greatly dependent on how you use these valuable tools.

To improve yourself, do everything you can to prepare yourself to accomplish your goals. As you focus on your most important goal first, embark on any self-improvement projects that will assist you in achieving this goal. If your goal is to enhance your productivity in order to increase your income, you will find it vital to begin with basic spiritual principles.

If you don't have an accurate and loving image of yourself, any self-improvement will be ineffective. You are your most important product. Only by recognizing your own special and correct value, will you be successful at valuing the things you do and the goals you achieve.

- Associate with friends who build you up properly. Participate in gatherings of people where conversation, instruction, and motivation are designed to improve people. Avoid negative people, places, conversations, activities, and thoughts.
- Refuse to descend into the attitude that you are too old, too young, too unskilled, or too unnecessary to succeed. Productivity and success are internal goal-seeking mechanisms. You cannot keep a mentally successful individual from succeeding. On the other hand, overconfidence can sometimes kill success, as well: "He who sits on mountain with mouth open waiting for roast goose to fly in waits a long time . . ."
- As you consider your most important goal or goals, assess and write down your strengths that will help you accomplish this goal. Assess and write down your weaknesses that will hinder you from accomplishing this goal. Plan ways to use your strengths. Plan ways to strengthen your weaknesses so that they may contribute to your success.
- Involve yourself in self-improvement programs that will strengthen both your strengths and weaknesses, especially those that will help you to accomplish the immediate tasks at hand and to achieve your most important and immediate goals.
- Practice your newly gained skills by volunteering and giving to others.

The "you" rule states: The more I know about others, the better chance I have of providing value. Nothing much ever happens until two people come together to effect an exchange or bargain. This is what commerce is about. This is what communication is about. Even relationships. A meeting! Sometimes when two people come together, nothing happens. At other times, everything happens. Sometimes more than everything happens. This is called synergy, the product of two or more people coming together is greater than the sum of the parts.

Just as the "me" rule deals with your personal side of the equation - the "me" side - the "you" rule deals with the other side of the equation. The more you know about and understand the other person, the better chance you have to create productive value: The better the chance you have to create a win/win situation where you both come out winners; the better the chance you have to create synergy where the result is better than winning! Where the result is genuine health, wealth, and freedom for all participants.

When you use the "you" rule, you will learn all you can about the people or businesses with whom you are interacting as you work to achieve your goal. People change every day: their interests change; their likes and dislikes change; their circle of friends and enemies changes; their activities, such as where they work and play and with whom, change. If you plan to meet with someone, it is best to try to do it on common ground. In order to find that common ground, you must know where the other person stands.

Businesses are like people. They change every day. If the successful achievement of your goal requires that you meet with a business and business people, then you must have current and accurate information about them. Businesses experience changes in the economy, technology, products, consumer acceptance, politics, and environmental impact, just to name a few. Business people get promoted, move, retire, and die. These changes create new opportunities. Opportunities are like open doors. If you don't know the current state of things with a business or with the people involved in the business, you may miss these opportunities, and the open doors may be closed to you.

- Your most important resources for getting to know people and businesses - for finding the open doors - is through the people you already know: your friends, family, and fellow workers. Ask them to be alert to information and opportunities that could be of use to you as you seek to achieve your goal.

- Seek guidance and wisdom through prayer concerning the things you would like to do.
- Keep in touch with former friends and employees. They know your skills and strengths and can easily open doors for you that otherwise might be closed.
- Read the newspaper. It tells you what is going on in your community and the world around you. It keeps you up to date. Read the "help wanted" and "business opportunities" sections in the want ads - *even if you already have a job*. You may find opportunities that become open doors. Read other sections in the want ads. The want ads are an open marketplace where a congregation of vendors offers a cornucopia of open-door opportunities through which possible "meetings" for commerce and exchange can take place.
- Join civic and professional organizations that can provide you opportunities to serve others as you seek to achieve your goal. The Chamber of Commerce, public service clubs, labor unions, hobby and craft groups, professional societies - all of these and many more will provide you with a wealth of contacts that may be of value.
- Become politically active. Working and rubbing shoulders with other people who are actively concerned about the condition and betterment of people, businesses, and communities is often an education in itself. It has been said that you can learn more about the upside and downside of other people in the political arena than any other place. But the key word in being politically active is *active*. As you seek to achieve your goals, you are free to act for yourself or to be acted upon by others. This freedom to act is much like the freedom in financial freedom. To be acted upon is much like financial bondage.
- Keep accurate records of all your contacts. These records can take the form of diaries, ledgers, note cards, or appointment books.
- Always acknowledge the help of others. Write thank you notes or letters to those who have helped you in any way. Always return phone calls. There are few things as

damaging as a courtesy ignored or a favor left unacknowledged.

Looking for a new job or position provides an ideal opportunity to apply the "you" rule strategy.

(1) Exactly what business is this company conducting?
(2) What are its main products or services? What are its important features?
(3) How long has the company been in business? What has been its growth record?
(4) Who works for the company? What kind of people are they?
(5) Are special credentials or training required to work for this company?
(6) What is their hiring procedure?
(7) What are the specifics of the job for which you are applying? What are the duties and responsibilities? What are the opportunities for advancement and self-improvement? What is the downside of the job?

The "24-hour" rule states: Everybody has the same 24 hours in which to work. There is no special dispensation of time given to successful people. People who succeed and people who fail use the same clock. But how each person uses the minutes and hours and days and weeks and months and years will in large part determine his or her success.

Even though we all have the same 24 hours in each day, there are things that steal time from us, depleting our usable supply: In the following list of "time thieves," rate them as no problem, a sometimes problem, or an always problem at stealing time from you.

________ (1) I procrastinate a lot.

________ (2) I have trouble making up my mind about things.

________ (3) I have to redo tasks because of mistakes or poor workmanship.

________ (4) I become frustrated because I try to do everything myself.

________ (5) I am often late for appointments.

________ (6) I usually don't have a plan before I start things.

________ (7) I find myself bored much of the time.

________ (8) I often have trouble finishing projects I start.

________ (9) I have too many irons in the fire.

________ (10) I allow myself too many interruptions.

Often, asking the right questions helps us find the right answers to problems in our lives. As you considered and rated the above list of 10 "time thieves," you were asking yourself questions about potential problem areas in the way you manage time. Perhaps you discovered that sometimes time manages you! Begin by making a plan to solve each of the "always" problem "time thieves." Then concern yourself with the "sometimes" "time thieves" problems. As you work to improve those areas where you are less successful managing your time, you will find yourself more able to enhance your productivity and increase your ability to handle money and other resources wisely. You will find more success in playing the game – to succeed!

Steps must be taken one at a time. This is the "focus" rule. As you begin enhancing your productivity and increasing your income, you will reach your destinations one at a time. If you have your sights set on too many different destinations at once, you will find yourself getting confused or even lost. It is important to focus on first things first. It is important to focus on the principles of spiritual faith, mind, emotions, will, and body. This will help you understand which of the things you desire are necessary to fulfill your life's destiny.

Setting priorities, working from agendas, using flow charts and program-evaluation-and-review techniques to better understand cause-and-effect relationships in our lives are the tools used by successful people to sharpen focus and do first things first. If you imitate these habits of successful people, you will find yourself imitating their productivity and success. Certainly round wheels work better than square ones, but you don't have to reinvent the wheel every time you use one.

The "right tool" rule states: Each part of my personality is a specialist. These special parts make up my productivity and success team. Each of us is unique, and we all have our own set of unique and very special tools that, when developed and used effectively, help assure success.

YOUR SKILLS

With every new activity or task, there are new things to learn. Learning means practicing, practicing means growing! Learning builds new skills, and new skills build new strengths. One of your most important tools is knowing how to learn.

- Two readings, two viewings, two listenings. Whether you are dealing with written material or video or audio taped material, two times through it is best. The first time through the material, concentrate on getting an overview of the subject. The second time, take notes and create an outline. This will raise your retention level considerably.
- If you can teach the material that you've learned within 48 hours of having studied it, your retention will go up even more. Find someone you can talk to about what you've learned, describing the high points.
- Develop a goal sheet of those tasks you want to accomplish based on what you've learned.
- Establish some accountability by taking a test or by being accountable to someone for the things you've learned.
- Review the material or your notes and outline. Periodic review of the material you learned will complete the learning cycle and raise your retention to the highest possible expected levels.

Yesterday's skills may fall short of tomorrow's challenges. As you read, listen, watch, and learn – your skills and abilities will grow. As you practice, your skills and abilities will become true strengths. Besides your reading, listening, and watching, consider (1) attending conferences; (2) establishing one-on-one contact with experts and mentors; (3) becoming good friends with your local library; and (4) apprenticing yourself out, without compensation. *First, become an observer, then become a doer.*

Before we can lead other people to help us accomplish worthy goals, they first must like us, trust us, and respect us. If a person doesn't like you or respect you and has no reason to trust you, he or she isn't going to buy what you're selling, whether it's yourself, a product or service, or an idea. Experts say that almost ninety percent of job failures stem from personality differences rather than from lack of skill or ability.

The single most important thing you will ever study or learn about is how the rules of life affect you! The single most important skill you will ever develop is the art of being friendly, in other words, the art of reflecting and sharing life's principles and genuine health with others. If you have unwise personality differences or conflicts with others, all the good work you do, or desire to do, to enhance your productivity and increase your income will be "left in the dugout." A healthy personality is one of the most important traits of productive and successful individuals.

The dictionary defines posture as "Your frame of mind; the position or attitude of your body ..." Your posture is one of the most important aspects of your "self." Good posture can help you to become a superstar. But posture is more than just standing up straight. It deals with all the aspects of your personality, both inside and out, as well as your attitudes and what people see.

Posture from the inside out works like this:

(1) Are you courteous to others? Are you willing to meet them at least half way? Are you genuinely concerned about their welfare as well as your own?

(2) Are you a creature of good habits? Are you consistent and dependable? Are you honest? Do you do those things that will make you a good neighbor? Do you always hold up your end of things?

(3) Are you organized? Do you recognize the importance of planning ahead to avoid problems and to realize the most from life's opportunities?

(4) Are you mentally and physically healthy?

(5) Are you a mentally positive person?

A major part of this posture is maintaining a "positive attitude." This means choosing to learn the rules that result in being positive. It means appropriately sharing your dreams with people. The best way to create synergy is to bring positives together. Read books, watch videos, and listen to audio tapes that reaffirm positive rules and values As you do this, you can become acquainted with the most "positive" minds in all the ages. Change your focus from self to others. This will result in greater positive energy in your life and the lives of others.

Now let's view posture from the outside in:

Experts tell us that you have exactly thirty seconds to make a first impression. This means that you have just thirty seconds to demonstrate your positive attitude, to make others feel comfortable in your presence, and to create an atmosphere for success. The difficult part is that we never get a second chance to make a good first impression. How do you answer the following questions?

(1) Are you outwardly healthy? Do you cast the appearance of good heath and good physical condition? Are you well groomed? Are you physically clean? Do you exercise? Do you control your weight, or does it control you?

(2) Is your speech effective and in keeping with your task? Do you use good grammar? Do you know what you want to say well enough to say it so that others may understand you and respond to your wishes?

(3) Is your phone manner gracious and professional? Does your phone voice and posture accurately communicate who you are and what you're all about to those on the other end of the line who cannot see you?

(4) Do you use the words thank you, excuse me, and please? Do people consider you to be a thoughtful person? Do you send thank you cards to those who have given you help along your way? Do you remember birthdays, holidays, and anniversaries?

(5) Do you have good manners?

(6) Do you stand up and sit straight? Does your physical posture reflect an attitude of confidence and purpose?

(7) Are you careful with the clothing you wear? A book is often judged by its cover. How does your clothing affect the first impression people receive of you?

While a book shouldn't be judged by its cover, your "cover" is still important both in how you are judged and how you feel about yourself. This is called "dress for success."

- Focus on quality rather than quantity. One or two outfits of good quality are a better buy and provide a better first impression.
- Consider cost per wearing. Paying a lot of money for an article of clothing that will be worn only a few times

increases the cost per wearing.

- Know the difference between fashion and fad. True fashion seldom goes out of style. With classic and basic items you can update your wardrobe quite easily. Fad purchases last only a season or two at the most.
- Be well pressed as well as well dressed. Being clean, neat, and well pressed can spell the difference in how you look and feel about yourself.

Finally, always remember that you live to succeed. Learn, and live by, the rules of life. Where enhancing your productivity and increasing your income are concerned, develop an active belief in, and acceptance of, true spiritual values, guidance and a healthy mind, emotional base, will, and physical body. This path to a totally integrated personality will result in a fulfilling life. This is how to successfully fulfill your life's purpose and regain your American heritage of financial fitness. What we are talking about is maximizing your quality of life. The next chapter gives you more practical suggestions for improving the quality of your life and the lives of your loved ones.

CHAPTER EIGHT

The Priceless Quality of Life

As America approaches a new century, an important new paradigm emerges that emphasizes a higher quality of life versus a greater quantity of things. Never have there been so many options available to us in our various spending areas. We must become informed regarding the options in each area in order to make wise spending decisions."

Unfortunately, much of our lives are occupied with acquiring and owning possessions and property. Each day we learn new rules that affect how we acquire and own things. As we use these rules in the economy of daily life, our attitude toward quantity and/or quality of possessions changes.

FINANCIAL FITNESS FACT # 8

"A life time measured by its quality rather than its quantity is a life span to be treasured."

These rules and our attitude toward them become our values and form our personal financial philosophy. They determine what is important to us and what is not as we bargain with life's changes. But, what determines which rule or values each individual will like and use?

Some psychologists who study the behavior of people try to quantify and list reasons why people do what they do. Unsurprisingly, many of these reasons fall into two general categories: people tend to prefer and repeat those experiences that make them feel good and tend to reject and avoid those experiences that make them feel not so good.

Of course, lots of superficial things make people feel temporarily good: things that taste, smell, sound, look, and feel good; things that make them feel accepted by others; things that make them feel important, things that make them feel secure, or more successful, just to name a few. And, as you look at your own life and your relationship to the people, places, and things around you, a few things that have temporarily made you feel good should come to mind immediately.

But there are other factors that help to determine what rules or values you like and those you don't. One of the most important of these factors is the paradigm: *what you believe to be true about the world around you becomes your "model" of how life is.* From birth, people, conditions, and circumstances have been convincing you that the world is naturally a certain way, that people naturally act a certain way, and that it is silly to think of the world or people being any other way because that's just the way things are! The way you believe things are has become your paradigm of life. Because of this paradigm, it may never occur to you that things could be any other way. This is the power of the paradigm.

The world is filled with many paradigms. There are large paradigms and small paradigms, and you may be affected by them unknowingly. Often, what others believe about the world around you has far-reaching affects on your behavior and on the rules or values that control your acquiring and owning of possessions and property.

One of the most important events that can change your behavior is the *personal paradigm shift*. This happens when you decide to start looking at the world in new ways. Perhaps you learn something new and important. Perhaps a person or condition or circumstance in your life makes a big impression. Suddenly, you start to look at things in a new light or as if through someone else's eyes. Suddenly, you no longer are willing to accept what you previously believed to be true and natural about the way things are. Suddenly, your model changes. Suddenly you undergo a personal paradigm shift. The following story illustrates how personal paradigm shifts occur.

> *The students at Thomas Jefferson High School considered one of their classmates to be very conceited. Often, he would completely ignore them when they spoke to him. Many times he failed to respond when someone asked him a question. It was as if he was*

above such nonsense. He would hold his head high and pass by as if others weren't even there. He was the talk of the school. Who did he think he was? Too good for them?

One day the stuck-up student appeared in school with hearing aids, one in each ear. Suddenly, everyone realized what had been happening. The boy wasn't conceited at all. He simply had not been hearing their comments or questions and was, therefore, unable to respond.

This created a sudden **paradigm shift** *for the students at Thomas Jefferson High. What they had previously believed about their classmate obviously was not true. They now understood the real source of the problem. This new understanding was a shift in their collective paradigm. It changed the way they acted and responded to their classmate.*

Both life's experiences and personal paradigm shifts can change the way you look at things. Major paradigm changes or "world view" changes can also affect your rules or values.

As a result of many factors, including the decline in spiritual values, major "world view" change has taken place in the last fifty years. During the two-hundred-year history of America, there have been many national paradigm changes. Periods of material conservatism have cycled with opposing periods of aggressive materialism where the ownership of possessions and property have been the chief concern. The Industrial Revolution, which made the manufacturing of necessary and luxury goods easier and faster, encouraged a new interest in "things" that could be owned, used, and enjoyed. The times that preceded this new era of manufacturing capability and "assembly line" prosperity had been marked by a scarce conservatism, when "things" had been made by hand, one at a time. The novelty of the easy availability of an abundance of "things" spurred an unbridled rush toward the accumulation of as much as possible. Many people found themselves going to excess, often spending themselves into financial bondage in their rush to own a "quantity of-things." Today the novelty of quantity has worn thin. More and more people have come to realize that the extravagance of past decades has not brought happiness. The pressures of the rat race and the evils of debt have caused many people to reconsider what is important to them. These evaluations have served to create **a major paradigm shift in the way these people look at things and what they value**. The following five points describe what these people have found:

- **A high-consumption lifestyle is less fulfilling.** Great numbers of the baby-boomer generation are feeling the desire to move in new directions in search of greater satisfaction and fulfillment in their lives. Many have found that they are not getting as much enjoyment out of the fast-paced life of the big city that was promised by the "spend and enjoy" slogan makers.
- **A "quantity-of-things" often leads to a high level of indebtedness.** With the easy-credit policies that manufacturers have employed to encourage purchase of their goods in greater and greater numbers, many of the present generation have found themselves mired in financial bondage. In recent years, the cost of credit has escalated alarmingly. Such excesses have caused many people to take a second look at whether or not they feel good about their way of life.
- **The "quantity-of-things" lifestyle strains family life and heightens personal stress.** It is well accepted that money problems are a major contributor to the high rate of divorce and the breakdown of the family. Easy credit and persuasive advertising have convinced many people that "shopping" is an acceptable form of social expression. But, when it is time to pay the bills, conflicts often arise. Tensions escalate between husbands and wives. Aggressive or erratic behavior often follows. Additionally, an abundance of labor-saving devices has caused many of the past generation to become the equivalent of "couch potatoes." This sedentary lifestyle has caused many people to neglect exercise and the practice of physical and athletic skills that, in the past, have helped people to maintain health.
- **We are ready for a change.** America is a cyclical coun-

try. Following the "Jazz Age" of the 1920s, America had a major economic depression. A major war followed this depression. A relatively long period of prosperity followed the war. During this period, the Judeo-Christian culture of America came under attack. A remake of the "Roaring 20s" followed. In each case, the excesses of the former cycle led to the beginning of a new cycle that reversed those excesses. The excesses of the present cycle, the cycle of heavy consumer spending and too much debt, have been going on too long and have become too extreme. The cyclical character of the American economy over the past fifty years indicates a change is on the horizon. New patterns of living are already developing. New lifestyles are being sought by more and more people. We are poised to make a quantum leap, which is the ultimate paradigm shift.

- **American spirituality is on the rise.** A resurgence of spiritual values in America, together with the advent of the new "information age," offers the possibility of a higher quality of life. The success of the industrial revolution was dependent upon the ability to produce virtually every product consumers desired on an assembly line at a lower cost than was possible in the old-style craft shop. It was the automation of industrial capability, with its production of inexpensive goods and the advent of the violation of sound financial principles, that lifted the "First World" out of the agricultural age into the industrial era. The computer is now accomplishing the same thing for the "knowledge revolution." It expands the ability to develop, store, recall, analyze, and process information and to draw better conclusions. At the same time, it encourages unhealthy consumerism, stressing the acquisition of material things at the expense of spiritual values. This lack of moral certitude and direction has led to runaway debt.

Part of regaining your American heritage of financial freedom means accepting that you need to make your own paradigm shift. Financial fitness and freedom means shifting from a desire for a "quantity-of-things" lifestyle to an active pursuit of a life filled with "quality." You will come to realize that possessions are merely tools to assist you in life's great adventure. Possessions are not goals to be achieved. This, together with the return to spiritual values, positions Americans for a major paradigm shift, one that will be characterized by cultural distinctions such as preference for quality over quantity and freedom from debt. Personal fulfillment achieved because of internally held high values is potentially much more rewarding than trying to improve and satisfy yourself by hanging decorations in your life, much as you would decorate a tree at Christmas time. The decorations are fine for the moment, but when they are no longer in place, the tree remains and must stand on its own merits. So it is with the things you own. In the world of tomorrow, the dictum of the Industrial Revolution that "more is better, big is great" may no longer be a choice. In all likelihood, life will be increasingly judged more by its substance than by its veneer.

It is a challenging task to assess your values with an eye to changing things, but yours is the power of choice. Only you can decide how you feel about your lifestyle. Only you can decide if there are things you will change or improve. Let's look at seven significant areas in your life that can be greatly affected by your major personal paradigm shift, by what you decide to believe and do: family, community, nature, health, education, the arts, and spirituality.

FAMILY

The family is the fundamental unit of all society. Historical accounts reveal that at various times the definition of "family" has taken on some interesting meanings, but families have always been a part of life on planet earth. At the same time, the quality of family life experienced by individual family members has ranged from good to not-so-good. The big question has always been, which is more important, the individual, or the family group?

Each person in a family is uniquely different and therefore entitled to special consideration. No one set of rules and circumstances is perfect for everyone. Each family member is an individual and stands alone and apart from all others. On the other hand, no family member is an "island." Family members must cooperate in various ways to survive in a world where competition and the law of the jungle are often the rule. In the family, there is strength in numbers. In today's world, where there are many forces working to redefine the traditional biological or nuclear family and family values, it is important for you to invest the time to understand your interests and to make your choices about what is important to you. Family members can get caught in the "rat race" of working to pay for homes, cars, and a "quantity-of-things" lifestyle, leaving little time to build a quality family life.

COMMUNITY

In many ways, communities are like extended families. The earliest communities often were formed from groups of closely related families or family groups. You are part of many communities: (1) a shareholder in the community of men and women who inhabit Planet Earth; (2) a citizen or resident of a nation, state, and city or town; (3) a member of a church, civic group, political party, club, or team. These are only a few examples of communities. The quality of your membership in these groups is largely a matter of how much you are involved and the strength of your commitment to each group. The degree of your involvement and commitment is largely a matter of your interest and choice. Likewise, the strength of each of these groups is dependent, in part, on how much you care and how much you do to support the community. When you think about how you relate to the concept of community, consider some of these questions:

- Outside of your family, what are the most important communities or groups with which you presently associate?
- Communities and groups are made up of "neighbors." Often these neighbors live next door, down the street, or in the same town. Some of our neighbors may reside on the computer "bulletin board." They may be fellow team members, committee members, or board members. They may belong to the same political party or the same church. They may belong to the same club. Who are your neighbors that you would like to know and support better in order to improve your community's "quality of life?"

- If you had complete freedom of choice, what areas of your present community involvement would you change?
- How would your increased or redefined community involvement improve your community's "quality of life?"
- What do you need to change in your life in order to enhance your community commitment and involvement?

NATURE

The pursuit of a "quantity-of-things" lifestyle often skews our vision so that we miss the importance and benefits of the natural world around us. In our headlong race to create a world of "things," we have abused nature. Many resources have been lost in the name of progress. Now many people are beginning to seriously question former ways. Preservation and conservation efforts are being advanced at every turn. Many people are beginning to realize that earth is not an endless storehouse of resources to be plundered.

As you look at your own life and your interest and attitudes about nature and its potential benefits to your own "quality of life," consider each of the following questions:

(1) When was the last time that you and those close to you found yourselves "... in nature's arms, beneath her canopy, touched by her gracious love?"
(2) What are your present feelings about the preservation and conservation of natural resources?
(3) What changes could you make in your life in order to be able to better care for and enjoy the world of nature, to improve long-term "quality of life" for you and future generations?

HEALTH

American health statistics are now among the worst in the industrialized world! A combination of harmful eating habits, denaturalized food, a more sedentary lifestyle, and destructive attitudes are to blame. We are bound by our fast-paced lifestyle that encourages "fast food," "instant" this and "instant" that, and "pre-cooked," "pre-processed," often almost "pre-digested" meals. Often we are more concerned about "looks" rather than "reality." If we have skin problems, we cover them up with cosmetics. If we have posture problems, we hide them with especially designed clothing. If we have body-conditioning problems, we alter our lifestyle to accommodate our infirmities. We take aspirin to ease the pain of headaches. We take drugs in the form of alcohol, tobacco, coffee, tea or hard drugs to cloak deficiencies in our lifestyles. We have become a nation of spectators, rather than participants. We'd rather watch our favorite team play than play on one. We'd rather ride our lawn mowers than push them.

Consider the following questions about your present lifestyle:

- What forms of useful exercise do you participate in on a regular basis?
- Do you feel that exercise can help you improve your "quality of life?"
- Do you feel that you could improve your present diet to enhance your "quality of life?" If so, what would you change?
- As you look at the portion of your budget that you presently allocate toward good-health concerns, what could you change to decrease this expense and, at the same time, improve the health of yourself and those close to you?
- When was the last time you spent time learning about ways to improve your health through reading, listening, or consulting with an expert?

EDUCATION

When you know how to do something, it's easier to make meaningful changes in your life. When you don't, you can become frustrated. This is a value of true education: knowing how the world works and how to work it.

Your desire to know more about how to be financially free is an example of how you have been motivated to become educated in principles that will help you attain your goals. That's what education is about: knowing more and doing something with what you know. Now, ask yourself how much time you allot in your life each day or each week for education, not just the accidental "bumping into" facts, but considered, meaningful education. Your answer, and what you choose to do about it, can make a big difference in your pursuit of an improved "quality of life."

Education has a big impact on your ability to change. Knowledge is a key to growth. Without it, you're weak, often at the mercy of others who have knowledge. But more importantly, you often are powerless to make the changes that will give greater meaning and enjoyment to your life and to the lives of your loved ones. The following questions will help you explore your attitude toward education:

- What do you feel are the most serious problems presently facing the education of our youth within our society?
- When was the last time you formally participated in a class or learning situation where you were accountable for what you learned?
- What were the most obvious results from your participation in the class or learning situation mentioned above? How do you feel about the effort you made at that time to improve your life through gaining knowledge?
- How do you feel about the amount of money you currently allocate within your budget toward educating yourself and those around you about whom you care?
- How could you use education today and in your future to improve your "quality of life?"

THE ARTS

The arts represent the "culture" of a society. The arts express its philosophy and sometimes its highest achievements. The "masterpieces" of human creativity and insight are often viewed as treasures of rare value as they have expressed man's desire to connect with his Creator. More importantly, they can represent the best efforts of men and women in the past who have looked "upward" and "inward" to gain understanding of the human condition. At the same time, they can provide unparalleled inspiration for those of us who experience them.

Art, music, literature, drama - these are the developments within human thought that can give coherence and perspective as we move from generation to generation. A personal involvement in the arts can add substance to your world view.

Exposure to art that uplifts the spirit will build character and virtue and will leave you with a sense of the richness and breadth of human experience as you develop and shift your personal "quality of life" paradigm. Here are some more probing questions that you should consider:

- When was the last time you participated in the arts by attending a play or concert, visiting an art museum, or reading a literary treasure?
- How would you describe your knowledge and sensitivity to cultural things?
- How would showing more interest in the arts improve your "quality of life?"
- How would showing more interest in the arts improve the "quality of life" of those around you about whom you care?

SPIRITUALITY

Where there is an absence of beneficial spiritual beliefs, society does not possess the "stuff" to sustain itself. Declining "spiritual values" foreshadow a breakdown within the social group. Some people have called spiritual awareness and sensitivity the "glue" that holds society together, the "meat" that gives sufficient meaning to life to justify its perpetuation as a grand and noble thing to be valued and protected.

Many people look to God as a Supreme Being who oversees all nature with benevolence and good will and has the power to set things right. Some look to other sources for their basis of spirituality such as the order and harmony of the universe; the inherent optimism of the human spirit that seems to triumph over evil and destruction; or the reliability of a causal world, where "effect" follows "cause" with apparent good faith.

In today's world of technical enlightenment and secular insight, "spirituality" takes many forms. In general, it recommends to people that they look to sources of inspiration and power outside themselves for comfort, enlightenment, and refreshment of the elements of "humanity" that make us different from the rest of nature.

This country was founded on the desire to live out the spiritual relationship and principles founded in the Judeo-Christian faith. The majority of debt accumulation in this country, and the unjust earning of wealth, has directly resulted from ignoring the spiritual foundation to these financial principles. The practical solutions in this book are designed not only to embrace these principles but help you incorporate them into your life so that you can enjoy healthy economic success, freedom from debt, and genuine financial freedom.

In your own life, spirituality can give coherence and meaning to all the other things you do. It can give perspective to the progressive generations of progenitors and descendants who (yourself included) will leave their legacy on earth and in the memories of generations to come. Here are a few questions to help you clarify your view of spirituality:

- At present, how important is spirituality in your life?
- How important is spirituality to those around you for whom you care?
- In your estimation, what would regular church attendance or consistent effort to nurture your spiritual nature do to improve your "quality of life?"
- Have you ever had an instance when you felt that you were helped through a difficult moment in life by some spiritual forces outside yourself?

As you begin to make new plans for the future, you will need to ask and answer many questions such as: (1) What is important or of interest to me? (2) Are these interests consistent with my spiritual beliefs and values? (3) How carefully will I spend my money and how informed do I need to be? (4) How does my income and other financial resources allow me to deal with "needs" and "wants?" Only you can answer these questions and the many others that will form the basis for your plan.

FOUR SPENDING AREAS

You may be surprised that four far-reaching spending areas where planning and care can have major impact on your life are among your most basic expense areas: food, health, housing, and transportation.

Food

Have you ever wondered how much of your monthly expenses go for food? The average American family spends almost

20 percent of its monthly budget on food: more than 12 percent on food eaten at home and more than 7 percent on food eaten away from home. It is no wonder then that putting greater effort into how you budget and spend your money for the food that you and those close to you eat will have major impact on your financial condition. The following suggestions will help you understand how you can budget and spend more wisely.

Consult with food and nutrition experts (through books, tapes, seminars, consultations, etc.) to learn the best advice about what you should eat and how you should buy it. There is a vast amount of literature available through libraries, magazines, newsletters, and public forums about food choices for better health and economy. In recent years, many experts have returned to the "simpler is better" point of view concerning food economy. Simpler foods are almost always more economical.

What you think of the food you eat is one of the most important aspects of your plan to improve your eating and spending habits. Study what the experts tell you. Consider their advice in the light of your own preferences and interests. At the same time, don't forget to consult with those who are close to you and with whom you share the dinner table. It may take time and experimentation to discover the food you and your loved ones can enjoy together.

Once you've gotten the best advice from the experts and from those close to you, compare costs of the alternate food choices. It might surprise you how much difference in cost there actually is between certain food choices. At this point, you are building a collection of possible alternate menus based on (1) cost, (2) nutrition, and (3) preferences.

Make a decision you can live with and like. Design your menu. Publish it. Display it. Talk about it with family and friends. Make it a working part of your life. As you do your shopping and prepare and eat your meals, be alert to better and better ways to improve your "quality of life." The condition of the human spirit often reflects the other aspects of our daily life in combination with the food we eat.

Keep things interesting. Nothing will shoot down your plan quicker than "meal boredom" or "rebellion in the ranks" from those who share your food. Always look for nutritious and economical ways of keeping things interesting. Your own resolve will suffer if you lose interest in your meal planning and preparation, if you forget that creativity is often the spice of life ... and dinner.

Follow through. The best laid plans are of little use if you don't put them into action. Be consistent. Paradigm shifts and lifestyle changes are marked by consistent differences in the way you think and act. If this is your goal, be honest with all you've planned to do. Give things a chance. The results are bound to surprise you. Changes in your "quality of life" will result from changes in the qualities and performance of your life.

The following suggestions could actually help you go through the process of change that stems from finding and trying new paradigms. Try them and see. Avoid impulse buying, use as few convenience foods as possible, avoid wasting food, watch out for expensive packaging (some packages cost more than the product), minimize junk food purchases, grow your own food, shop in bulk, and finally, create a food-storage program.

Health

Health care costs for the average American family have become a major concern. These costs can consume a large percentage of the budget. Any steps you take to better deal with this expense will have far-reaching influence on your financial freedom and your "quality of life."

Your health and the health of those close to you involve two concerns, health maintenance and health repair. The human body is a marvelous creation. It is easier and less expensive to maintain a body in good running condition than it is to repair one that has broken down. In our fast-paced society, it is often easy for us to disregard or forget about the maintenance of our health until the warning signals flash and the alarms go off. Then we're stuck with expensive repairs. Along with the high cost of doctoring poor health come the pain and suffering and the inconvenience and lost opportunity that always accompany illness and health breakdowns. Ben Franklin's adage that "a stitch in time saves nine" may be the truest where your health and the health of those close to you are concerned.

Health maintenance. There is no great mystery to maintaining good health. Good health and "feeling good" are the end results of correct living. These measurements tell you that you've been doing things right. The problem is that your marvelous body is often so good at adjusting and covering up for mistakes caused by an unhealthy lifestyle that sometimes you don't know you have a problem until the problem is critical. Often, poor health derives from chronic poor health practices. Symptoms can surface much later in life when they are more difficult and much more costly to correct if they can be corrected at all. Your life is a precious gift. The very substance of your life, and certainly your "quality of life," is largely dependent on your health.

The challenge of good health maintenance is based on a few simple principles: (1) a sacred respect and appreciation for your spirit and body; (2) wholesome nutrition; (3) proper exercise; (4) responding promptly and effectively to your body's natural cycles and needs; (5) avoidance of things that can hurt you or cause your body to break down; and (6) regular checkups by qualified health professionals.

The challenge of good health maintenance involves three steps:

(1) Learn all you can about your body and what it requires to be in the best running condition.

(2) Learn all you can about nutrition, exercise, your body's natural cycles and needs, and what is harmful or destructive. (Sounds like a major project, doesn't it? Just remember that you don't have to know everything at once. Your body has a remarkable ability - up to a point at least - to compensate for your ignorance and mistakes. Unlike your automobile or desk-top computer, your body is actually able to fix itself most of the time.)

(3) Also, remember that the learning process should be ongoing. Regular checkups with your doctor, dentist, and other health professionals will keep you informed and up-to-date. Time changes things. Regular maintenance checks are vital to a successful health maintenance program.

Learn whatever you can, whenever you can, as much as you can. Make it a life-long process and habit. Everything and anything you learn about good health, and good health maintenance will benefit you in the long run.

Another important part of good health is "working at it." Once you've consulted the experts and assessed your own body's needs, you must make a decision about what you are going to do about health maintenance. You must follow through and be consistent. Giving your body sporadic or incomplete attention will only frustrate your efforts to improve your "quality of life." And you must keep it interesting. The "boredom rule" applies to your health maintenance program. Keep the program meaningful and fun so you won't be bored into turning it off.

If you want to consistently feel good, you need to have a plan and use it. As we've said, "To fail to plan is to plan to fail!" You must learn to budget and carefully spend your "life resource," your good health. To fail to do so may leave you "bankrupt" where your good health is concerned. Your financial freedom can be seriously threatened by poor health and the need for health repair.

Health repair. For most Americans, health repair costs are the fastest growing major item in their budgets. Government at all levels, social agencies, health care professionals, health care consumers, all are gravely concerned with solving this serious problem within our economy. As you deal with your health repair needs and possible future needs at the personal level, you must take the same studied approach that you've learned to use in all your purchases. Get as much product information as you can, compare costs, think "quality," and buy for the long term. Additionally, it may be useful to inform yourself about the issues involved in the on-going national health care debate and to involve yourself in the process. By engaging yourself in this far-reaching assessment, you will become a smarter consumer. Smarter consumers, guided by spiritual principles, as a rule are more financially free and have a higher "quality of life."

Housing

Housing costs are usually the largest expense item the average person or family must deal with in the budget. In today's world, a home purchase customarily involves a long-term mortgage, substantial debt, and a lifetime commitment. The other alternatives of renting or leasing involve a major commitment of resources and a dependency on the whims of a landlord.

Each of these solutions to providing suitable housing for yourself and for those for whom you are responsible has potential for greatly affecting your "quality of life." Studies show that the average household spends more than 30 percent of its disposable income for housing. Because of this, how you allocate your funds and resources in dealing with the question of housing is probably a major concern to you.

Buying vs. renting. Many people face the dilemma of whether to buy or rent a home. Traditionally, there have been great benefits in owning real property, including your own primary residence. Owning real property can qualify you for special tax breaks. There is a sense of achievement associated with owning your own home, although in many cases "ownership" comes down to making payments on a long-term mortgage.

Renters and lessors, on the other hand, avoid many of the problems associated with home and real property ownership. Homes require considerable attention and maintenance in order to preserve them as the valuable assets they are. Unless leases or renter's contracts state otherwise, responsibility for maintenance and repairs rests with the property owner. Under this arrangement (1) tenants simply make their payment as agreed to, (2) use the rented property in a reasonable and responsible fashion, (3) protect themselves against any pertinent liability they might incur while resident at that location, and (4) insure themselves against any possible loss of personal property. With the tax breaks the government allows, the cost of housing tends to favor ownership, but the ease of movement and the limited responsibility associated with renting or leasing are sometimes more important.

When considering housing decisions always remember your "quality of life" is a function of your life's purpose. It all comes down to what you choose. The choice is yours. But, whatever choice you make, you should try to make an informed decision. Your own confidence in that decision, and your peace of mind, become major factors in whether you feel good or not-so-good about where and how you live. Friends, neighbors, the schools your children may attend, the church where you may worship - these and many other factors will be affected more by how than by where you live.

The future of housing. The rising cost of housing may be attached to standard inflation or any number of other factors tied to "supply and demand." Assuming business as usual, there is no reason to suppose that this trend will not continue within society. Occasionally, local factors cause the price of housing to go down, but in the long term the trend has been upward.

Currently, the cost of housing has leveled off. Some economists predict that during the coming decade this trend will prevail and that home prices and rents will not expand as rapidly as they have in the recent past. Some experts even predict that home prices may significantly decline. There are two important reasons for this: (1) Fewer people are entering the home-buying market. Since the population surge of the "baby-boomer" generation, there has been a slow decline in the number of births in America. This will tend to create a condition where supply exceeds demand; and (2) Changes in our attitude toward debt and the high cost of credit may create caution on the part of the upcoming generation when it comes to buying a home; many newcomers to the home-buying market are effectively being priced out of the market by the high cost of credit and the already-high home prices. This may cause the price of single-family homes to go down, while at the same time place a greater premium on apartments, condominiums, and other lower cost multiple-family dwellings.

Another important factor in the future housing market will involve where people live. Since the beginning of the Industrial Revolution, there has been a cyclical pattern to the movement of people to and from the city. At times, there has been greater interest and pressure to move to a rural setting. At present, there are indications that a trend toward rural movement is underway. The desire on the part of some people to get out of the "rat race" and to "get in touch" with a more natural setting is driving many people away from the city and into more rustic settings. This will affect housing prices in the city and the country, if the trend persists.

If the way we do business doesn't change, however, we will likely see the trend toward country living reverse itself as people move back to the cities. This is because at present cities are where most of the jobs are. Factors such as the computer revolution could force a fundamental change in the way we do business and could cause a major divergence from traditional employment patterns, but such possibilities are just on the horizon at this time. Nevertheless, as you consider where and how you will live in the future, you must be watchful and responsive to these changing trends. Your home and where you live and your "quality of life" will doubtless be affected in the very near future.

Even before the beginning of the 20th century, architects, social and city planners, visionaries, and others have speculated about the shape of the house of tomorrow. Houses hold a unique position within society because they stand as symbols for families and other similar groups. The nature of the family or group and the "quality of life" the group enjoys is often represented by the house where the family or group resides. It often reflects the group's character, ambitions, and dreams.

In recent decades, the traditional "house" has become less and less the focus of family activity and identity. Many forward-looking people see this trend continuing, with the house and home adjusting to changing social pressures to become even more a "way station." Such way stations would be places where family members with varied and often dissimilar interests and activity-calendars would pass one another for a few moments of family togetherness and interaction.

They would then quickly move on to a broader world of theoretically expanded focus, networking groups, and opportunity outside the home. Others see the role of the house and home expanding, becoming better able within the confines of its own walls and hedges to accommodate a full range of family, work, and social activities. Here outreach would take the form of excursions down the electronic highway, to name one example. Whichever vision is closer to the truth, the house of tomorrow may be much different from the house of today in many ways.

We may see houses that have different rooms and "room-mixes" from today's. The living room, parlor, family room, and kitchen may be replaced with an "us" room or "great" room that reflects and accommodates the expanded variety in family members' tastes but that simultaneously encourages convergence. Such rooms may actually reduce the effective living space of the house, eliminating waste, and at the same time decrease construction costs. In-house lap pools, exercise rooms, saunas, and spas may reflect an interest and emphasis on good health. Greenhouse rooms, hydroponics gardens, and atriums may reflect a back-to-nature attitude and an interest in home-grown food. Electronics and media centers, and in-house offices may accommodate a technological future where the information highway becomes a more important window to the outside world. Building lots may become smaller, with more efficient use of space. Houses of the future may be located in smaller defined "village" units. Non-polluting bicycles may become the preferred means of travel. Heating, cooling, and electrical supplies may rely on the sun.

Whatever your house of tomorrow looks like - whatever its floor plan, whatever its cost, wherever it is located - it almost assuredly will continue as a major symbol and factor in determining your financial fitness and your "quality of life." The more intelligence and care you use in determining its design, function, location, and cost, the more beneficial it will be.

Transportation

Have you ever wondered how much of your monthly income you spend on transportation? The national average is more than 20 percent. Twenty percent of your income just to get from here to there, just to "get around." If there ever was an area in your budgeting that could stand careful scrutiny, it is what you have allocated for transportation. And primarily this means the use of the automobile. If you're like most Americans, the car has become a necessity as well as a status symbol and source of identity. In recent decades the trend has moved toward automobiles that are either very large or very small, very elegant or very sporty, and generally very complex while very trouble-free. They have become reflections of high fashion, creating images of power, prestige, beauty, and intelligence. Certainly, there are other forms of transportation that may impact your budget, such as trains, planes, buses, and bicycles, but the automobile is the most expensive and has the greatest impact on your "quality of life."

How can you adjust your attitude about automobiles and

their place in your "quality-of-life" future without seriously compromising the lifetime of images you've amassed while the car has been so much a part of your life?

Don't make problems where they don't exist. If, after careful assessment and soul searching, you decide that you may have been heading down the wrong road with your automobile, then by all means make the adjustment. And, of course, the only way you can do that is to make an automobile paradigm shift.

Whatever you find offensive about your automobile, find its counterpart. Make a plan for incorporating it into your new outlook. Work the plan. Follow through and be consistent. With care and effort, this major expense area of your life will better comply with your desire to improve your "quality of life."

The next time you consider a car purchase, do it the smart way. This means finding the right car for your needs. A smart-looking sports car, while impressive to look at, may not be appropriate if you have a family. Make sure the type of car you are buying is right for your expected driving conditions. See how all the family fits in the car before buying. Study reports that compare more than one automobile.

Decide in advance what you can afford to pay for an automobile. Know the maximum cost as well as what you will pay in monthly payments. Become familiar with approximate operating costs, such as gasoline and maintenance. Look into insurance and registration/licensing costs. Be sure these are programmed into your budget. Never purchase a brand new car unless you pay cash and plan on keeping it for five-plus years. Let someone else pay the initial depreciation on your new car. It will save you thousands of dollars.

If you choose to finance, be sure to compare interest rates the dealer offers with those that can be obtained elsewhere. Never finance a car for more than 36 months. If you can't afford that payment, scale down to another car or, better yet, don't finance at all.

THE KEY TO LIFE QUALITY

If not me, who? If not now, when? One final note. All the reading, all the studying, all the contemplation in the world will not be enough to change your life. Even a desire for a quality-based lifestyle filled with purpose is not enough. It all comes down to "action!" You must want to have a better life more than you want anything else in the world. Change, achieving a truly meaningful reason for living, must become a driving, almost all-consuming part of your daily existence. Only if you seek a real sense of renewal, only if you get in touch with the miracle that the Creator unfolds each day, can you begin the journey to self fulfillment. Financial fitness and health do not occur in a vacuum. They are part of an entire living discipline, a commitment to gaining the most you can from every aspect of the wondrous adventure of living. You are a spiritual, mental, emotional, and physical wonder. Accepting this fact, while at the same time honoring the great mystery that life presents each day, is key to changing your future. But you must desire to be all that you were born to be. The choice to become, to achieve your fullest potential, to live each day of your life completely and with absolute reverence is yours. Choice! Choose to make the first move. Realize that the journey to regaining your American heritage of financial freedom is a significant part of that choice. Ask yourself if you have the will to achieve your success. Remember, wishful thinking is simply fantasy. Write down your goals and your plans to achieve them. Then pray for guidance and begin the journey with a vision for your ultimate success.

A life lived in this way will be a joyful celebration. To be sure that your success plans extend into your retirement years, read on.

CHAPTER NINE

The Golden Years

From the beginning of civilization, men and women of advancing years have moved, or been moved, from the active work force to a dependent status when they were no longer sufficiently productive to provide for themselves or for those under their care.

The 20th century has brought a new dimension to retirement. With adequate planning and preparation, men and women in the workplace now are able to voluntarily withdraw from their labors before their time of interdependency in order to enjoy the fruits of labors performed earlier in their lives. This is retirement as most Americans know it today.

In this modern era, many people look forward to retirement as the attainment of the American Dream. They hope for an idyllic time when they no longer need to work, being able to put aside the careers they have pursued for most of their adult lives. In anticipation, retirement often represents a time when men and women can embark on a new and vital phase of life, one filled with new opportunities, enlarged interests, new friends and associates, and new fulfillment. However, for many people retirement represents a time of uncertainty and struggle. It may be a time when their ability to satisfy life's basic day-to-day needs may be in doubt. It may be a time when the dream loses much of its luster. Often this difference between anticipation and realization depends on the extent and quality of planning done in preparation for this important new phase of life. **If you fail to plan wisely, then you plan to fail.**

FINANCIAL FITNESS FACT # 9

"Based on 1992 statistics, only 4 in 100 Americans were financially prepared to retire at age 65."

Retirement offers many challenges and choices. The key to effectively facing these challenges and making beneficial choices during your retirement is the planning and groundwork you put in place before it is begun.

The key to experiencing a workable and enjoyable retirement is planning, preparation, and living consistently with your life's purpose. One of retirement's greatest prospects is the potential freedom it offers you in fulfilling the final stages of your destiny. It can be the time you are most free to live your life with new patterns of fulfillment. But you must engage in thoughtful, spiritual, emotional, psychological, physical, and wise financial planning. Planning like this will give you confidence and an opportunity for genuine freedom. A secure tomorrow is one of the greatest benefits of waking up, becoming financially fit, and regaining your American heritage of financial freedom.

There is no single set of plans that will help you prepare for your retirement. You are unique. No one else has your life's purpose, hopes, expectations, or experiences. Your circumstances, wants, and needs are unique. Your goals are your goals alone. Only you can determine how you will achieve them today, and in retirement.

You must begin today to engage in thoughtful future planning. You must identify your wants and needs and develop plans to achieve them. Then you must continually review and revise your plans as you gain new knowledge and experience. You must define your projected retirement lifestyle and prepare yourself emotionally, spiritually, psychologically, physically, and financially to obtain and maintain it. As you make your plans, you will come to know yourself better today. You will also come to know what kind of person you want to be tomorrow, in retirement. You will come to better understand the resources within yourself and your community to help you realize those options that are most desirable to you. The more you begin to plan and anticipate your retirement, the more your attitude toward the future will become positive.

Change is everywhere. It is a ruling principle in your life. In order to live with it, you must understand it and build that understanding into your plans for the future. The best place and time to begin to understand how change will affect you as you plan and prepare for your retirement is today. Getting to know just who you are right now will help you to understand what changes might affect your plans for retirement.

A valuable exercise is to ask yourself "who am I?" You can do this by making a list of your likes and dislikes, your skills and training, your personal relationships, your job, your goals, and how you spend your leisure time. After writing down your present personal profile, project yourself into the future and ask the same questions from the perspective of who you would like to be.

By the year 2000 projections indicate that the over-65 age group will consist of 30 million people in the United States. Society is already shifting from an emphasis on youth to one favoring the interest and values of mature adults. These changes need to be considered as major influences affecting your definition of retirement and your retirement plans.

It has been further estimated that by the year 2000 the life expectancy of women will surpass 84.5 years and that of men's will be greater than 80 years. This means that the new "middle age" group with be made up of youthful and vital 50 and 60 year olds. As you approach your active retirement years, you need to consider the many changing roles that a shift in emphasis in your life will bring. Many new roles will come with retirement. However, you will not assume them automatically. You need to learn about them and learn how to incorporate them. This takes practice. As you begin to make plans to assume these new roles, your expectation will increase and your attitude will become more positive about the prospects available to you through the changes that will accompany your retirement.

Your retirement should begin with a positive, expectant attitude that your role changes will work for you. As you develop such an attitude, make up your mind to be happy. Get involved with the people who will affect your retirement. This could be considered your support network. It includes your family, friends, neighbors, colleagues, clubs, and community and religious groups to whom you are attached and upon whom you rely for support in day-to-day activities.

As you look to your retirement, you need to assess the individuals within your present support network to determine who are likely to remain and who are likely to disappear. For example, in retirement, you won't be able to interact in the same ways with your former circle of friends from work. You may find it necessary to make new friends. Preferably, this should be done before you retire. Good planning includes deciding how you are going to adjust to role changes.

Retirement can place a strain on marriage relationships in ways never expected. More time together requires adjustment in the attitudes and roles of both marriage partners. Here are several important factors that couples should consider:

- Plan your retirement together; be mutually supportive.
- Help each other to rediscover old friends and find new ones.
- Discuss finances candidly. Work together to plan and agree on your retirement budget.
- Exchanging and sharing some household chores could stimulate marriage partners to create new ways of thinking about their various new roles and help them to understand each other better.
- Develop new activities and routines. At the same time, one of retirement's greatest joys is the freedom to make spontaneous decisions.
- Respect each other's privacy. You both need and deserve your own personal sanctuary.
- Keep up your appearance. A good appearance suggests self-respect and respect for your partner.
- Above all, marriage partners need to communicate with each other. Talk! Share plans, problems, hopes, and dreams.

Your retirement preparations should include plans for the possibility that your marriage partner will not always be there. Candidly discuss the possibility of each other's death and prepare for it, and note whether the planning includes the following:

- A will or a family trust for each of you.
- A joint plan describing all assets, their location, and how they are to be distributed in the event of death.
- Realistic estimates of income and expenses for each surviving spouse.
- A list of professional advisors to assist with decision making and emergencies.

- Information about widowed persons' support groups that can provide emotional support should the need arise.

Of course not everyone who retires has a partner. Single living is a satisfying first option for many people, whether throughout life or at a particular stage of life. Single living may offer many advantages in retirement, including the freedom to come and go as you wish and the freedom to choose your own friends and interest. The disadvantage may include lack of companionship and in-home support.

Retirement is often expected to bring more freedom, more privacy, and more discretionary money. However, you may suddenly find yourself with new responsibilities that can affect your freedom and finances. Circumstances such as caring for an aging parent or assisting an adult child can have a serious impact on your plans. The need to assume such roles in the middle of retirement is not unusual and should be planned for.

Retirement plans should include preparations for unexpected circumstances. The feeling you have toward your parents, siblings, and children should be clearly addressed to lessen the burden of dealing with or assisting them should the need arise after you are retired.

It's good planning to strengthen all family ties so that no one person needs to bear the burden of helping others within the family. This includes planning how you can balance your needs with the needs of others in your family.

You are only as young or old as you think you are. Retirement can provide you with many opportunities to interact with young children and teenagers. Forming connections with young persons may help you discover fresh ideas and new interests. You and the young friends you make will benefit from shared experiences. Volunteering for school activities and recreational activities, or assisting with organized youth groups, will help you to keep a young perspective.

It's been said that you never actually retire, you just shift emphasis. This shift can be a gradual process or an immediate transition. However, it culminates in the moment when you leave your job or profession. In this regard, there are some commonly held myths associated with retirement that can be considered as you approach the time of making the decision, "When should I retire?"

(1) Myth number one. Hold on to your job as long as possible. This concept reinforces the idea that retirement from your job is necessarily a bad thing, to delay as long as possible. It is good to continue doing things that bring you fulfillment, but there may be opportunities or interests that make the decision to keep working at the same job as long as possible a foolish one. Weigh your options mindfully, wisefully, and prayerfully, and then decide.

(2) Myth number two. Retire at the earliest moment. Some people try to embark on a lifestyle that vaguely resembles retirement before they are really ready to retire. Quit too early and you may miss the opportunity to bring to your vocation the wisdom, maturity, and experience that mark the years of most people's peak effectiveness. You may miss out on the most rewarding years of your working life.

(3) Myth number three. Retire when you're fed up. Every once in a while, a job gets to be too much for us. But individuals who jump into retirement because of temporary dissatisfaction discover that this may be the poorest reason of all to retire. They miss out on friendships, financial considerations, and the benefits of carefully planning for this important shift in life.

(4) Myth number four. Give the youngsters a chance. Some studies have shown that if we extend retirement to age 70, it could create a hardship for new individuals entering the work force. Some believe this could cause unemployment in many fields. However, your decision to retire should not be influenced by something so external as these arguments. Your decision should be based on your life's purpose and compatible needs, desires, and interests. It's the only way retirement will work for you.

ARE YOU READY? A CHECKLIST

Are you ready to retire? Here's one approach that can help you test your perspective on making plans for eventual retirement. This will get you started, eventually you may want to construct your own test or find a test that better reflects your own value system. Check the one statement in each group that most closely agrees with your situation according to the principles you are learning in this book. The checklist on pages 144-145 will give you some idea about whether or not you are ready to retire from your present job or to shift emphasis.

The many factors affecting your retirement need to be taken into consideration. Each action may be independent, but they need to be considered together. For example, you may be ready in all areas but one, which by itself could make early retirement a catastrophe.

Here are three suggestions that may help you make the necessary preparations and adjustment to be ready for retirement:

(1) Prepare for retirement, don't let them retire you. When an individual feels that he is unprepared to take an action, it becomes less easy to take it in the right frame of mind. Don't retire from the job, retire into something.

(2) Regard retirement as a promotion. This promotion is a new phase of your career. Look at it as a phase wherein you can win greater satisfaction and rewards, materially, spiritually and emotionally.

(3) Be excited by the opportunity. Look at the positives associated with retirement. It's easy to see possible problems, but the benefits can be very rewarding. The freedom of thought and action that awaits you when you have properly planned and prepared for your retirement is part of an exciting adventure.

Your health will play a vital part in helping you to achieve a successful and fulfilling retirement lifestyle. As you lay plans to keep yourself spiritually, mentally, emotionally, and physically fit, you will build a foundation for enjoyment whatever your age.

Many of today's health problems are the result of lifestyle choices: poor diet, smoking, lack of exercise, stressful living, and abuse of alcohol and drugs, to name a few. On the other hand, choosing a lifestyle that includes good nutrition, exercise, rest, and a positive mental attitude will go far toward solving many potential and existing health problems.

Begin your planning for a healthy retirement with a visit to your physician. Once you have checked with your doctor, you

FINANCES

____ I don't have enough financial reserves on hand to make it right now.

____ I have enough money to scrape by, but I'm not sure about inflation.

____ I can make it if I live cheaply and cut back on extras.

____ I'm okay for the foreseeable future at my present level of income.

____ I will do fine with my finances in almost any situation.

____ Money is no consideration.

HEALTH

____ My work keeps me zipping along, gives me exercise, and forces me to watch my diet and personal habits.

____ I feel that my work favors my health in that it keeps me busy and on a regular schedule.

____ My work generally leaves me dragged out at the end of the day. If it weren't for weekends, I'd be in a bad way.

____ My work is a terrible strain. It drains my energies, keeps me on edge, and doesn't let me sleep at night.

RELATIONSHIPS

____ If I retire now, I suspect my personal relationships will suffer badly. For example,
I suspect my spouse and I will get on each other's nerves and I will lose some of my job friends and so on.

____ I'm not sure if I have enough friends, or good enough friends, to give me a satisfactory social life if I stop working.

____ I've never depended very much on people I met on the job for socializing, and I have a well-rounded group of friends and relatives who always have given, and will continue to give, me a full social life.

____ The minute I stop working, I'll be able to improve and devote more time to practically all of my relationships.

EMOTIONAL OUTLOOK

____ I'm emotionally unprepared to stop work. If I retire now, I won't be able to make the many adjustments that are necessary.

____ I don't believe retirement is going to be much of a threat for me. I'm pretty flexible in my emotional outlook.

____ I find the prospect of retirement exciting and offering all the appeal of an exciting adventure.

____ I can hardly wait for retirement. There are so many things I want to do.

HOUSING

____ If I stop now, I'll have to give up my present living arrangements for something much less desirable.

____ My retirement won't affect my housing arrangements much one way or the other.

____ I expect to receive benefits from my retirement: I'll be able to do a lot of work around the house that I've been putting off for years, which will mean not only enjoyable activity but also an increase in the value of the place.

____ If I retire now, I'll be able to move to another site and residence that will give my whole life a lift.

WORK

____ I would miss work terribly. There is so much more that I want to achieve before I quit.

____ Work? I can take it or leave it.

____ I'm proud of my work record. However, I feel that I've achieved about all I'm going to accomplish

____ The day I leave the job will be one of the happiest days of my life.

ACTIVITIES

____ I know I'll never find anything else to do that I will enjoy as much as I enjoy my job.

____ I enjoy my life on the job as much as anything I might do on the outside.

____ I like the idea of getting on to new things.

____ There are any number of things I've been eager to do, and when I leave my job, I'll finally have enough time to get to them.

can look into fitness and wellness programs. Various clinics, senior centers, the local Y, and other community groups often have programs especially designed for those wishing to enhance their retirement lifestyle through healthier living. They often have specialists that can help tailor a program designed just for you.

Your body changes with advancing years. Some forms of exercise and play that may have been appropriate for you at a younger age may no longer be suitable for your retirement years. However, many seemingly difficult forms of exercise may be introduced into a daily or weekly workout schedule if you start slowly. An appropriate exercise program will offer a variety of rewards that can strengthen your heart and lungs, increase your flexibility, curb your appetite, relieve stress and anxiety, help you sleep better, keep you mentally alert, improve your appearance, create an internal sense of well being, and help protect you against illness. As you seek counsel regarding an acceptable exercise program, make certain that you address all the exercise needs of your body and engage only in programs suitable to your needs. Don't go overboard or overdo things.

The best exercise programs are rhythmic. They should be continuous and vigorous. For example, brisk walking, bicycling, swimming, and dancing will suit most needs very well. To be most beneficial, exercise must be at least 20-30 minutes in duration and be engaged in at least three times a week. Try to alternate your exercise days for best results. Make your exercises gradual and progressive. Work with sufficient intensity to increase your pulse rate, to draw perspiration, and to make you breathe deeply. Each exercise period should include 5-10-minute warm-up and cool-down periods. Light calisthenics, stretching, jogging in place, and stationary bicycling are good warm-up and cool-down activities.

The secret to retirement eating and drinking is that you continue to need the same nutrients but fewer calories. Retirement meals should be designed with this in mind. A balanced diet should not require vitamin and mineral supplements. It is a good idea to cut down on certain substances in your diet, now and in retirement, including fats, sugar, salt, and caffeine. At the same time, a balanced diet should contain fiber or roughage.

Special conditions may require special diets. For example,

osteoporosis may afflict postmenopausal women. This is a degenerative disease that causes a reduction in bone mass caused by calcium deficiency. It can be prevented by assimilating adequate amounts of calcium and by exercising. The recommended daily amount of calcium for postmenopausal women is *1,500 milligrams*.

Alcohol consumption can affect nutrition. Some studies suggest that moderate drinking may aid digestion, relieve stress, and stimulate the coronary arteries. The majority of studies recommend elimination of all alcohol consumption. As people age, their bodies change the way that alcohol is metabolized. The same amount of alcohol tolerated when younger may become a problem later in life. Alcohol contains no nutrients, and heavy drinkers often skimp on meals. Also, mixing alcohol with certain medications can create serious problems.

Maintaining a satisfactory weight can become a challenge in later years. Often with decreased activity weight seems to magically escalate. If you need to lose weight, lose it slowly but steadily. Don't eliminate foods from the basic food groups but cut down on your portions. Curb, or better yet eliminate, your intake of alcohol and sweets. Follow your exercise program carefully.

Stress is part of daily living. We all experience it. Without it, we can't expect much change in the world for good or bad. However, unmanaged stress can cause a lack of concentration, irritability, fatigue, loss of appetite, chronic anxiety, and depression. Untreated severe stress can lead to ulcers, hypertension, and heart attack or stroke.

It is important to determine the level of stress under which you work the best. Recognize stress. Admit that you are feeling it.

- Identify the cause of stress. It can come from some surprising sources, both positive and negative.
- Take some kind of action to relieve your stress. Decide what you want to do, then act. Indecision is one of the worst stress producers.
- Accept the fact that you can't control every situation. Some things are simply beyond your control.
- Exercise is a great stress reducer.
- Rest. Fatigue makes even small problems loom large and

inconsequential pressures seem as if they can flatten us.

- Avoid self-medication and potentially abusing substances. Pay attention to the good advice of experts.
- Laugh more. It is the second best stress reducer in the world, especially when you are able to laugh at yourself.

THE STRESSFUL BIG 10

(1) Marital separation
(2) Death of a close family member
(3) Personal injury or illness
(4) Marriage
(5) Getting fired
(6) Retirement
(7) Marital reconciliation
(8) Going to jail
(9) Death of a spouse
(10) Divorce

The following stress test on page 149 is one of many testing approaches that can provide you with perspective on how stress may be affecting you. This will get you started, but eventually you may want to create your own test or find others that more closely reflect your personality, situation, and lifestyle.

Write in the sources of stress from the "Stressful Big 10" in the order you believe they would most affect you. Then circle those stress events that you have experienced in the past 12 months.

Those stress events that you have circled are called "stress points." They have caused you stress over the past year. Add their mean value. If your score is **over 300** you are in a high-stress condition. A score of **200-300** means you have a better than average chance of suffering a stress-related illness within the next 12 months. A score **below 200** indicates low stress and a life that is interesting and healthy.

Retirement is the tenth highest stress point in people's lives in America. As you make your plans for retirement, learning to manage stress should become a high priority.

You are the one responsible for most of your health. You are responsible for becoming more aware of your body's needs and recognizing any changes or early warning signs of poten-

Stress Event		Mean Value
(1)	______________________	100
(2)	______________________	73
(3)	______________________	65
(4)	______________________	63
(5)	______________________	63
(6)	______________________	53
(7)	______________________	50
(8)	______________________	47
(9)	______________________	45
(10)	______________________	45
(11)	Change in health of family member	40
(12)	Sex difficulties	39
(13)	Addition of new family member	39
(14)	Business readjustment	39
(15)	Change in financial status	38
(16)	Death of close friend	37
(17)	Changing line of work	36
(18)	Change in number of arguments with spouse	35
(19)	Overextended mortgage	31
(20)	Foreclosure of mortgage or loan	30
(21)	Change in responsibilities at work	29
(22)	Son or daughter leaving home	29
(23)	Trouble with in-laws	29
(24)	Outstanding personal achievement	28
(25)	Spouse beginning or stopping work	26
(26)	Beginning or ending school	26
(27)	Change in living conditions	25
(28)	Revision of personal habits	24
(29)	Trouble with boss	30
(30)	Change in work hours or conditions	20
(31)	Change in residence	20
(32)	Change in schools	20
(33)	Change in recreation	19
(34)	Change in church activity	19
(35)	Change in social activity	18
(36)	Obtaining a mortgage or loan	17
(37)	Change in number of family get-togethers	15
(38)	Change in eating habits	15
(39)	Vacation	13
(40)	Christmas	12
(41)	Minor violations of the law	11

tially serious health problems. If you need to see a doctor, be an assertive patient. Be prepared when you see your doctor or health provider. Be ready to describe your symptoms accurately, to provide all relevant background information, and to discuss all medication you are taking. If you have doubts about treatments or procedures, let your health care provider know. Ask about alternative treatments, side effects of drugs and procedures. Ask about costs. Write down all the questions you want answered and insist that they be answered in language you can understand. Remember: You are entitled to a second opinion if you think one is merited. Preparing yourself to deal with all of these suggestions can be a major part of your retirement planning in the health and fitness areas.

RETIREMENT ACTIVITIES

Time, as it is in all phases of your life, is important in retirement. The use of time can become extremely valuable to self and others. Because of the shift in emphasis during retirement, many old activities will be put aside. New pursuits must be defined and brought into a regular agenda. Because of this, an important goal of retirement planning is to identify your special priorities and needs regarding the use of your time and to find activities that will achieve them.

An early estimation of how much retirement activities will cost should also be an important part of your planning. You may have an abundance of time during retirement and a wealth of ideas about how to use it, but if you have little money with which to make the best use of it, you may not be in the most desirable of circumstances. Most people need an appreciable level of involvement and a sense of doing things that are of value. Persons who age the best tend to be involved in a variety of meaningful interests and activities with many people.

The following is a list of activities that may become important to you during retirement. It represents only a beginning but may assist you as you contemplate your plans for the future.

Crafts and Hobbies

Among other things crafts and hobbies can represent a practical way to help others develop character, skills, and knowledge while serving as an outlet for the creative sides of our natures. Working with crafts and hobbies often allows us to be involved with a particular creative project from start to finish. (Being able to affect the entire activity, as is usually the case with our crafts or hobbies, can be a very fulfilling experience.) Often, we seek after such activities outside our work experience as a means of relaxation and refreshment. During retirement, such activities can become our total preoccupation as we have fun and make meaningful contributions to others.

Continuing Education

Adults everywhere are returning to the classroom in record numbers in a variety of settings: high schools, colleges, universities, trade schools, correspondence schools, libraries, museums, televised classes, and various specialized centers. It's never too late to develop the skills and gain the knowledge needed to fulfill our purpose during each stage of our lives.

Travel

Travel takes you outside yourself and involves you with seeing the world and interacting with other people, places, and things. Travel can expand our interests. There are so many fulfilling advantages to travel. Travel can be short-term or long-term, near or far – it really doesn't matter. The key factor is your use of time, means, and interests in accordance with your life's purpose.

Contemplation

You may find that having time just to look calmly and quietly at yourself and the world around you can be one of the greatest advantages to retirement. The accumulated wisdom you have gained from life can be placed in more meaningful perspective if you use this period in your life to also "take time to smell the roses."

It is important that each of us continues to grow personally, emotionally, and spiritually. Your retirement plans can include creating special times and opportunities for contemplation. It is important that such activities don't enter your life as strangers when you begin your retirement.

Sports

Beginning or continuing to participate in various sports

and athletic activities during your retirement may be an important means of health maintenance and social contact. Group walking, hiking club activities, aerobics, aqua-aerobics, golf, tennis, bowling, swimming, and ballroom dancing are all excellent examples.

Participating from the gallery may also be an excellent retirement activity. Often, one's interest in sports can be served as well as a spectator if physical or financial limits prevent personal participation in a particular activity.

Volunteering

Volunteering for service in various ways around your community can assist you in making the adjustment from your busy work schedule to a more leisure-time schedule during retirement. Volunteering can provide a sense of identity, self-worth, being needed, and productivity. Volunteering can be of great benefit to you and to your community.

In your retirement you should consider the value of volunteering, even if you do it for only a few hours a day or week. As you form your retirement plans, laying the foundation for a productive volunteer effort in your areas of interest will be a big help. It is important that you do what is meaningful, purposeful, and brings joy. Consider what experience you have had and how this might apply to the needs of the community. Every talent or skill has a volunteer application. Ideally, volunteering should be a mutually beneficial relationship. As you contribute your talent, time, and skills, others benefit and you continue to grow as a person. At the same time you are gaining new skills, interests, friends, and experiences, you are continuing your inner growth.

Many communities have volunteer centers or clearinghouses. Look for talent banks with various organizations. Because of the value of volunteering to your church or community, the comprehensive programs already in place will help you as you form your retirement plans. Consult with those who are already involved.

WORK IN POST RETIREMENT

The change in career emphasis offered by retirement will provide you an opportunity to do your best work, but the challenges are equally impressive. How you use your time will greatly affect your state of mind and contentment. Make specific plans in advance so that you can optimize your retirement experience. This amazing time is your opportunity. Use it as if it were the most valuable time in the world.

Your options during retirement provide interesting challenges. You may elect to continue working at your life-long occupation beyond the traditional retirement age. Or you may decide to re-enter a new area of the work force after being retired for a while. Many people use retirement as a time to launch a business of their own. Any one of these options, or a combination of them, may be the answer for you. Only you can decide. This time is as important or perhaps even more important than any other time in your life.

What do you have to offer?

As you retire from your life-long job, one of the most interesting decisions you may face is whether to continue working, either full or part-time. If you decide that your circumstances dictate that you continue to work, you may face the challenge of convincing a prospective employer that you can add value. The question that you will be asked is, "What do you have to offer?"

It is a good idea to take a good look at yourself to determine just what you do have to offer as part of planning for retirement. You should be aware that you may have to sell a prospective employer on the reality that, as a group, retirees today are healthier, more active, and have a longer life expectancy than ever.

Special contributions retirees can bring to a job include (1) maturity and flexibility to deal with serious and challenging problems in the workplace (maturity and flexibility developed during a lifetime of dealing with problems, crises, and change); (2) reliable basic work skills; (3) "people" skills; (4) "character" skills such as loyalty, conscientiousness, reliability; and (5) stability skills developed in the highly competitive and demanding give-and-take school of the workplace.

Once you have made the decision to work in one fashion or another during some phase of your retirement, the next step is to approach the prospect as deliberately and efficiently as possible. You may be able to get an employment agency or community service group to give you support in this effort, but much of what you will accomplish in finding suitable work during retirement will come through your own efforts and ingenuity. The following suggestions will give you an outline of steps you could take to accomplish the task:

Size up yourself. You must look at yourself honestly! What are your strong points? Where are you weakest? What are your assets? What are your liabilities? If you were the employer looking at you as a retiree as a prospective employee, what would you see? In a practical sense, you become the product you are trying to sell, so determine what the features of this "product" are that will translate into benefits for a specific employer.

Define your goals. It all comes down to your purpose in life, wise planning, and acting in accordance with the rules in life to carry out that plan.

Size up the job market. Once you know what you're looking for and what you're best suited to do, you are able to assess the existing job market intelligently. A place to look is where the majority of non-entry-level jobs are found in the network. Talk to former co-workers, supervisors, and employers. Try to establish connections through relatives, acquaintances, and friends. Use the resource facilities of religious, community, and service organizations. Read professional and trade publications. Consult the Chamber of Commerce and the business section of the newspaper. Pray for guidance, work smart, and be diligent in your search.

Using the network. Often, the best jobs are found by word of mouth. As you widen your circle of acquaintances, make the most of these contacts. Conduct informal interviews with as many people as you can. Discuss the field or fields you are considering as retirement work opportunities. Use such contacts as a source of information, not a job. Through this process you will narrow down job opportunities that are both attractive to you and available.

Be assertive! There are two key steps in the interview process. First, you must secure the interview itself. Until a prospective employer has decided to interview you, you'll never get a chance to present your product, yourself. Role playing at earning the interview will help you. Friends and family can help you answer questions most likely to be asked (ones you discovered during your job market assessment).

When you're satisfied that you're ready for the interview and have made an appointment, now comes the second step, presenting yourself. The goal is to make your valuable qualities clear to your potential employer. Consider the content of your answers, body language, and overall appearance. Display an energetic, interested image and personality. Give the potential employer every reason to want to hire you. Be on time, use a firm handshake, speak clearly, use eye-to-eye contact. Send a thank you note following the interview.

Closing the deal effectively! Remember, nothing happens until an agreement is reached, even when you are presenting yourself. When the job offer or offers roll in, be prepared to close the deal. This means being ready to discuss salary and other benefits. Before hand, you'll want to have collected current information about wages and salaries for similar work. Be prepared to suggest a pay range. Then be prepared to convince the offering employer that you're worth the upper end of the pay range.

Setting Up Your Own Shop

A viable alternative to seeking employment is starting your own business. There are many kinds of businesses that could work well for you during your retirement, if setting up your own business is a good idea in the first place! Too often the lure of being your own boss clouds many serious issues that must be considered before a positive decision on setting up a business can be reached.

- Do you have a good idea for a business? Is it one that answers a reasonable need in the marketplace? Is it one that has a chance of making money?
- Do you have sufficient energy and good health to meet the considerable demands of running a business, even a small business?
- Do you have sufficient commitment and patience to ride through the down times that often mark business start-ups?
- Do you have sufficient money, or a money source, that will

allow you to capitalize a business start-up successfully and carry it through to profitability, often a period from three to five years?

- Do you have adequate business skills such as bookkeeping, sales, product control, management, and so forth?

Once you have answered the preceding questions to your satisfaction, then there are some things that all successful business people do before building on the faith that starting a business requires:

- Form a good business plan. Without one, you won't know where you want to go with your business or how you're going to get there.
- Perform research about your business idea, the marketplace, marketing strategies, finance strategies, and so forth. These will help you form your business plan and to make mid-course adjustments as required. You can't know too much about these aspects of business when going into business. If you're going to run with the sharks, it helps to know how to swim like one.
- Get good legal, tax, financial, and insurance advice. The pros depend on the pros to take care of these concerns.

Always remember there's nothing like going broke, but there's really nothing like going broke during retirement, wiping out the preparations and savings of a lifetime for what can be wonderful years.

RETIREMENT LIFESTYLE – HOUSING, LOCATION

As you plan for your retirement, you will need to consider your lifestyle in both the present and the future. What is important to you? How will you spend your time? How active are you? How important are your friends and will they change during retirement? Will your lifestyle change if your spouse is no longer with you? Is hospitality important to you? How important will employment, educational, social, medical, cultural, and recreational opportunities be to you? How will your present lifestyle preferences change?

A necessary corollary to your lifestyle during retirement is where you will live and the kind of housing that will suit your lifestyle needs. For instance, during retirement, it may be important to have medical facilities close at hand, as well as public transportation and shopping.

Look at your current home. Ask yourself some questions. Will it suit your needs during your retirement both early and later on? How about upkeep? Is it energy efficient? Is it safe? Will you be able to handle taxes, insurance, and maintenance? Will it be affordable?

Look at your neighborhood and community. Will they continue to meet your needs during retirement? Will they require you to make compromises or tradeoffs?

If you own your home, it probably represents a valuable asset to you now and likely will continue to do so during retirement. The equity that is present in your home consists of its cash value minus any claims against it. In order for you to realize actual monetary benefit from this asset, you will need to carefully evaluate the benefits and disadvantages of different equity conversion scenarios offered at the time of your retirement. Some of these may include the following:

- **Reverse Mortgage.** When a home is owned outright, or when sufficient equity is present, the equity may be paid back to the owner in monthly payments. Terms for such a loan will vary depending on interest rates, the equity you're borrowing against, and length of the loan. Payments are made in various ways or when the homeowner dies or sells the home.
- **Sale or leaseback.** Such arrangements are also known as "life tenancy arrangements." In this scenario, the owner sells the property to an investor, retaining the right to live in the house as a renter. The investor pays the owner in monthly installments over an agreed-upon period and covers such obligations as home insurance, taxes, and repairs. Usually the investor will purchase a deferred-payment annuity for the owner that provides the owner with continued monthly income once the house has been paid for by the investor.
- **Deferred payment loan.** Such loans are usually provided to low-income people at a low interest rate by a local government. It permits homeowners to defer payment of principal and interest until the homeowner dies or the house is sold.

- **Homeowner equity accounts.** These loans, which allow the borrower to borrow against a portion of the equity in property, are being offered by brokerage firms and banks nationwide. They allow the owner to set up a line of credit secured by a lien against the home. The owner can draw on this credit using a credit card or by writing a check.

The major drawback to using your home as collateral for a loan is that this could endanger this important resource. Good legal, tax, and financial advice is important. Additionally, the sale of a home after retirement has special and specific tax considerations as well as benefits that could directly affect your retirement finances. Consult with qualified financial advisors before making a move to sell property after your retirement. It is prudent to proceed with the best advice possible.

If, after your lifestyle review, you decide that you want to change housing or location, use the same method to review your housing options that you used to examine your lifestyle. Some of the options available to you are a single-family home, a home within an adult or retirement community, a manufactured or mobile home, a condominium, a cooperative or shared home or apartment, a rental, or lifetime-care housing that provides room, board, recreation, and medical care.

Many questions should be asked about housing and location before you move. Consult with experts and those living nearby and under similar circumstances. Spending time collecting information so you can make an intelligent decision about a prospective move is much easier than being disappointed by the move and being faced with relocation. You will likely be working with limited or fixed resources after retirement. Depletion of these through less-than-careful actions could be devastating to your long-term retirement plans.

When making plans for retirement housing, location, and lifestyle, it's a good idea to make these plans with your spouse, if you are married. Often each partner has entirely different ideas about these critical elements in retirement. Imagine your surprise when plans you've made unilaterally and privately turn out to be in conflict with your spouse's.

RETIREMENT FINANCES

Just as with your present finances, retirement finances boil down to income and outgo. Also, just as now, you cannot long survive if outgo exceeds income for any extended period of time. Virtually every goal you make while planning your retirement has the potential to be affected by the money in your life. **One of the primary reasons for becoming financially fit and financially free is to have adequate resources during the precious years of your retirement.**

Income

The first rule in planning your finances for retirement is that the same rules apply then as for the present. The exercises you have learned (and hopefully have begun practicing) through reading this book will assist you as you make plans for your retirement. However, there are special considerations worth noting. Wage-earning is probably your primary source of income now, but during retirement, pensions and profit-sharing plans, Social Security, investments, savings, and part-time work are more likely to provide the sources of your income. As part of the paradigm shift discussed earlier, it is important to know that some of these sources of income may not support your values and purposes.

The following is a brief description of some of these sources of income. The descriptions reflect current programs. But it's important to realize that these programs are constantly changing.

Pension and Profit-sharing Plans. Take time to get to know your pension plan. What happens to your pension under various scenarios for retirement? Any decisions you make that affect your long-term future in retirement will be affected by the terms of your pension. Failure to understand and work within these terms could be harmful to the success of your retirement. Your pension is your retirement income. Don't gamble with it now.

Do-It-Yourself Pensions. All persons who have income from work can set up an Individual Retirement Account (IRA). Many employers offer a 401(k) plan that you can use, if you so choose. Self-employed persons can set up a Keogh plan, plus an IRA and a 401(k). Each of these plans is an example of a do-it-yourself pension.

Such do-it-yourself pension plans may help you in three ways: (1) If certain conditions are met, part of the income you put into these plans may not be subject to tax; (2) interest or dividends earned by money put into these plans may accumulate tax free during your working years; and (3) you may be in a lower tax bracket when you start drawing income from these plans.

Tax laws affecting do-it-yourself pensions may change. Consult with qualified investment and tax advisers regarding the terms of investment, the amount you can invest, and conditions affecting withdrawal. Your employer may have rules affecting your pension that may take into account any do-it-yourself pension you set up.

Social Security. You can't talk about retirement without mentioning Social Security. In 1950, Social Security represented 50% of retirement income for persons in the United States During the 1990s, it will represent less than 30% of retirement income and will continue to be a declining share. The hard fact is that retirees in the future will be able to depend less and less on Social Security as a source of money.

Social Security benefits are available to you at age 62. If you retire before age 65, you will receive a smaller monthly benefit. If you continue to work after you begin to receive Social Security benefits, you will lose some or all of your benefits under certain conditions. If your income from various sources exceeds a certain amount during retirement, you may have to pay taxes on your benefits. Your local Social Security office can explain how Social Security can work for you. Also, you may ask for a statement of earnings that will show the Social Security earnings credited to your account to date. This record should be verified every three years.

Investments and Savings. Investment and saving are ways of putting present money to work so that it will "earn" money for the future. There are two ways of putting such money to work: lending (making investments) and buying (creating asset equity). The following are examples of these two ways of putting your money to work:

(1) **Debt or money market.** When you lend money, you can reasonably expect to receive interest on this money sometime in the future. The following are examples of put-

ting your money to work in the "debt or money market:

- *Treasury and agency securities.* These are investment securities or opportunities backed by various agencies of the U.S. government, including in some cases the U.S. Treasury. They include issues from such agencies as Federal National Mortgage Association (FNMA), Federal Home Loan Bank Board, Federal Land Banks, and U.S. Savings Bonds. They are considered by many people to be highly safe investments.
- *Corporate bonds.* These investment securities are offered by many companies and vary considerably in their quality and rates of earning returns. Such securities are graded according to their financial backing by bond-rating services, the highest rating being AAA and generally offering lower interest yields. The market price of corporate bonds fluctuates.
- *Municipal securities.* These are tax-exempt bonds offered by municipalities and states. Usually they carry lower yields than taxable bonds. They are rated as to quality, much as with corporate bonds, and their value may fluctuate over the years. Such bonds provide little or no tax benefits to lower tax-bracket investors, but may assist you if you are in a high tax bracket.
- *Savings plans.* Such plans include pass-book savings accounts, certificates of deposit (CDs), money market accounts, and interest-paying checking accounts. These accounts are offered by banks, savings and loans, and credit unions and are insured by the federal government.
- *Money market mutual funds.* These funds are investor "pools" that invest in a variety of investments, such as those listed above. Most such funds are not insured, and their yields can fluctuate daily. Many have "check-writing" privileges.
- *Annuities.* An annuity is a contract sold by a financial institution or insurance company that guaran-

tees the buyer a fixed income from the contract for a certain period of time, often for life. Such investments provide a steady income and freedom from managing your investment capital.

(2) **Equity market.** The second way to put money to work is by buying something that has value or equity. You hope that what you buy can be sold for more money than you paid for it. Also, you hope that whatever you buy will generate income along the way, such as dividends from stocks or rental income from property. The following are examples of equity buying:

- *Stocks.* When you buy stock in a company, you are buying a piece or "share" of ownership in that company. The value of your equity usually increases or decreases depending on the profitability of the company, although other factors may apply. Stocks may pay dividends from profits or profit sharing. Stock may be (1) preferred, which means they have a more generous and assured dividend but not as much growth potential as common stocks, or (2) they may be common and range from highly speculative to highly conservative.
- *Mutual funds.* These funds allow you to invest in stocks in a diversified way. You are able to buy shares in a professionally managed fund that invests in various kinds of securities. Each fund has its own goals and philosophy, which may range from conservative to speculative in terms of how it invests your money.
- *Real estate.* You can invest in real estate on your own or as a member of a syndicate or investment group. Any real estate venture involves risk; because of this, it is wise to consult with experts at every stage of the investment process.
- *Commodities, metals, gems, and collectibles.* Such investments are very speculative and have the potential for great loss as well as gain. The investment involves placing a "bet" on the future value of such things as pork bellies, corn, precious met-

als, and foreign currency. Your money earns no interest, dividends, or rent from such investments. Your return depends entirely on the value of the investment at the time of sale.

Some of the things to consider in evaluating each investment opportunity are (1) what are the funds used for, (2) what is their yield, (3) their safety, (4) their liquidity, (5) what guarantees and insurance do they offer, (6) their terms of investment, and (7) their inflation hedge, or in other words, how the value of your investment will keep up with inflation.

Outgo

The expense side of retirement planning depends on a careful analysis of what you are spending now and a thoughtful projection of how that will change by the time you are ready to retire. Also, inflation must be taken into account and adjustments made for it. A careful review of your projected lifestyle changes will help. Also, it is good to make contingency plans that allow for the loss of one's spouse.

Expenses may be broken down into "day-to-day expenses" and "big-ticket expenses." Day-to-day expenses are the routine, essential items needed to sustain your life in an acceptable and comfortable fashion during your retirement. Such expenses also include necessary large expenses such as health costs, funeral expenses, and so forth. Big-ticket expenses are optional items such as a European tour. These optional expenses can be estimated for the future, based on today's costs, and entered into your tentative retirement budget. The main consideration is to cancel the expenditure if cash is not available at the time.

The following list of major retirement expenses are based upon brief descriptions that may or may not be applicable for your purpose in life. They are listed as information and each one should be evaluated based on values, spiritual principles, and their purposes for your life.

Housing. Chief among your major retirement expenses is housing. As we discussed earlier, there are many variables affecting your retirement housing costs. These variables and their potential impact on your retirement plans emphasize the importance of arriving at a clear picture of what you want your retirement lifestyle to be. Some of the variables may be raised by a comparison of purchasing new retirement housing versus maintaining or renovating your current housing so that it will be suitable for your retirement. Also, as previously discussed, geographical location may have considerable impact on your retirement housing budget.

Medical and dental expenses. Increasing age may bring the prospects of higher and often more catastrophic heath care costs. At present, your best hedges against the future and your retirement are the various health care plans and insurance available through the government, insurance companies, and facilities such as Health Maintenance Organizations (HMO).

Medicare covers about 40% of health care expenses for retired persons. Supplemental health coverage may be available to you during retirement through your employer's group health insurance. This should be investigated. Health Maintenance Organizations usually cover most office visits and hospital expenses for a set fee, although you must often choose a physician from a list of doctors participating in the program.

Miscellaneous insurance. Continuing protection for your automobile, home, and personal property and continuation of public liability and health insurance will be just as important to you during retirement as now. For as long as these factors are a part of your retirement, you will need to have protection against calamities that could immediately exhaust your retirement funds. Of course, if you no longer own an automobile, then auto insurance will no longer be a factor.

Transportation. The question of whether to use private or public transportation will need to be answered as part of your retirement plans. Also, should you choose private transportation, questions about how many automobiles you should try to own and maintain during your retirement, their quality, and size will need to be answered. Any decisions you make should be discussed with anyone else whom they might affect.

Food, clothing, and personal items. It is likely that during retirement you will be living on a fixed income. This may require that you learn and use various cost-cutting devices and systems in order to make your expenses for food, clothing, and personal items as small and consistent as possible: using discount coupons, generic brand products, shopping during special sales, and buying in bulk, for example. These devices may already be part of your shopping strategy. If not, learning how to use them before the need is thrust upon you when you begin living on a limited or fixed income should be an important part of your retirement planning.

Travel, entertainment, hobbies. Special pricing and discounts are often available for "senior citizens." As you plan for your retirement, becoming aware of such devices as "two-for-one" prices and "off-season" and "off-hour" pricing and learning how to use them may be important.

Gifts and contributions. Determining your future policy toward gift-giving and contribution should be an important part of your retirement planning. Birthdays, Christmas, and other gift-giving seasons may cause frustration and hardships for retirees with large extended families and many friends and acquaintances. As you estimate your retirement means and budget, such considerations must be taken into account to avoid embarrassment and such problems as the appearance of giving favoritism.

Other kinds of contributions, such as to charity or to your church, need to become part of your retirement plans. Whatever your attitude toward such contributions and continuing such contribution, your future efforts need to be balanced against your projected ability and circumstances. You may be able to devise ways to contribute time and personal service instead of giving through ways that diminish your limited retirement resources.

Family assistance. Family, parental, and grandparental responsibilities never end. Where possible, contingency plans to assist a child, grandchild, or other family member in time of need or in an emergency should be part of your preparations for your retirement future. Additionally, you should build and foster a realistic outlook that acknowledges that circumstances can change and that you may not always be readily able to contribute monetarily to family needs as you may have done in the past. Again, you may be able to foresee and plan non-monetary means to contribute to your family in times of emergency or need, such as personal service or volunteering your time.

Parental care. It is entirely possible that you could be faced during your retirement with the need to care for one or both of your parents, or the parents of your spouse. These possibilities need to be taken into account as you plan for your retirement. Discussions with doctors and extended care facility administrators, as well as with insurance agents, could prove valuable in making these plans. Also, considering those with whom such expenses might be shared, and even making agreements with them, may be important to your long-term retirement security.

ESTATE PLANNING

Your "estate" consists of all your assets, plus anything that is owed to you, less anything you owe someone else at the time of your death. The proper management of your resources is important to you during any phase of your life. If you are going to have a dependable retirement "nest egg," it is of prime importance that you manage your resources with an eye to your future. If you are going to be able to leave a significant estate for your heirs, it is equally important that you manage your resources with an eye to their futures, as well.

When you die, your estate becomes a legal entity. You can influence the distribution of your estate through instructions regarding assets, payment of debts, and resolution of your personal matters. If you die intestate, meaning that you leave no instructions, the laws of the state in which you resided will determine how your estate is distributed. Good plans and workable instructions regarding your estate are best set forth in proper legal fashion: this is known as a will or trust. Identifying your assets and debts and leaving proper instructions for their distribution is known as estate planning.

Planning your estate should consist of two main areas:

(1) Identifying your assets and debts and setting up conditions surrounding them that will permit you to manage them during your retirement and direct their distribution after your death in the most effective and cost-efficient way.

This area of preparation requires that you understand your present financial situation, your future needs, and the needs of your heirs and that you make any necessary adjustments to accommodate your goals of "effectiveness" and "cost-efficiency."

(2) Establishing your will or trust with clear and legally binding instructions so that your estate and other details can be handled according to your wishes.

This area of preparation requires that you define just what you want to accomplish now, during retirement, and after death.

Estate planning is best accomplished using the team approach. This team could consist of your lawyer, tax accountant, banker, insurance agent, and financial planner. A spiritual advisor may also be an important part of the team.

- *Lawyer.* This member of your estate planning team can counsel you on your estate planning options and prepare all the necessary documents and see that they are properly signed and witnessed.
- *Tax accountant.* This team member can help you identify your assets and minimize your estate tax liabilities by, for example, providing information on tax breaks after retirement.
- *Banker.* Your banker can help you with overall financial advice and in setting up trust arrangements.
- *Insurance agent.* This team member can help you with your life and health insurance needs, as well as your liability, homeowner, automobile, and personal property insurance needs. The purpose of these various kinds of insurance is to protect the value of your assets.
- *Financial planner.* This versatile team member may be able to advise you on all aspects of your estate: taxes, investments, insurance, trusts, etc.

RETIREMENT RECAP

The following checklist will assist you in assembling a clearly written recap of retirement and estate planning records. Couples should consider assembling a joint recap and set of records. This recap will assist either spouse, children, family, heirs, or anyone assisting with care or estate resolution to deal with or dispose of your financial or personal matters.

- Full legal name
- Social Security number
- Legal residence

- Date and place of birth
- Names and addresses of spouse children, and parents, and death certificates for those who are deceased.
- Location of your will or trust
- Location of birth, marriage, divorce, and citizenship certificates, or the actual documents themselves.
- List of employers and dates of employment
- Education and military records
- Requests and preferences for burial
- Names and addresses of close friends, relatives, doctors, lawyers, and financial advisors
- Religious affiliations and records
- Memberships in various organizations
- Sources of income and assets
- Social Security and Medicare information
- Investment income records
- Insurance information on all policies, including life, health, and homeowners
- All bank account information
- Location of safe deposit boxes
- Location of all real estate with records and deeds
- Copies of your most recent income tax returns
- Current liabilities
- Mortgages and other debts
- Credit card and charge account names and numbers
- Property tax information
- Location of jewelry or valuable family possessions.

According to the U.S. Census Bureau the following breakdown represents the primary sources of income for retired persons :

30% Social Security
49% Pensions, annuities, dividends, interest, rent, and gifts
20% Earnings from work
01% Supplemental security income and public assistance.

Only 4 Americans in 100 can actually afford to retire at 65. This statistic alone should be reason enough for anyone to want to start now to become financially fit and free from debt. Don't be a statistic: **regain your American heritage and its promise of financial freedom.** In the next chapter you will see how wise investment can help you achieve your goal of financial fitness.

SAVING BOND
STOCK
INVESTMENT
IRA ACCOUNT
DEED

CHAPTER TEN

The Capital Idea

The future prosperity and security of our nation depend upon more Americans regaining their heritage of financial freedom and becoming empowered to take advantage of the unparalleled blessings of our free enterprise system.

The financial fitness principles that we've discussed in these pages represent a unique proactive philosophy that when applied diligently, with dedication, determination and faith, will guide you to financial independence. The key to your success in this life-changing endeavor is realizing the importance of taking responsibility for your own financial affairs.

Also, you must recognize that environmental conditions will help or hinder your effort toward financial freedom. More and more Americans realize that while much needs to be done to improve America's financial parade, more freedom prevails in the free enterprise system than in most other systems. American capitalism is recognized and celebrated as one of the most progressive and encouraging economic systems in the world.

FINANCIAL FITNESS FACT # 10

"Responsible stewards of wealth are America's brightest financial hope for the future"

Ideally, capitalism is the economic system in which private wealth, acquired lawfully under just and moral laws by private enterprise under free competition, is controlled by its owners. Although there have been great injustices during its first two hundred-plus years, which must be corrected, America has risen from a primitive base to a nation that produces one sixth of the world's goods and services. The genius of our constitutional free enterprise system, and the encouragement it has given to millions of Americans to be *responsible financial stewards*, fuels the vision for America's return to freedom from debt.

In America we are more free to use accessible resources to produce and provide goods and/or services to markets ranging from local to world-wide. The boundaries on our enterprises are societal structure, capital, raw materials, our own intelligence, wisdom, industry, imagination, and good citizenship within the context of morality and statutory law, and the effects of competition. *This is the vision of free enterprise.* Continuing to create an environment that permits and encourages this system to flourish and prevail in the marketplace for all people is the genius that will allow America to continue as the world's premiere productive economic force.

The concept of private property is the cornerstone of the capital-based free enterprise system. Undoubtedly, the greatest economic debate that has waged since the beginning of civilization has focused on the ownership of land, real property or real estate: Should our planet be considered the common gift of nature to be owned in common by all people? Or should land be parceled to individuals, under certain common laws and conditions, to be owned privately? This debate has carried individuals, communities, and nations into conflict and conciliation, war and peace. The myriad legal systems that have prospered and declined throughout history have been significantly influenced by laws of property. Economically, wealth and standing within the community have been determined, often almost exclusively, by the ownership of property. On the other hand, experiments where the common ownership of property has been advanced generally have ended in frustration. The failed push for world-wide communism is one example.

Responsible entrepreneurs realize that as we justly individualize ownership of property, we truly become responsible for it, and we improve it. As men and women have added their labor to property, the value of property has become a combination of the pure land value and the labor that has been added. Since that labor is private, very quickly the value of the land has become based more on the added value of human labor than on its original value. Thus, it has been reasoned that because of this, men and women have the right to withdraw land from "common" ownership and to treat it as "private" property.

The value of private property has come to be synonymous with wealth. Likewise, maintaining or improving its value is treated with the highest respect by society. The following three aspects of property will tell you something about why it is important to be a responsible entrepreneur:

(1) **Financial health raises the common good.** Private property is not entirely "private." It is part of the landscape and domain. It is part of the resources of the planet, part of the original gift. Because of this, communities often feel some sense of ownership and responsibility for private property. Zoning laws may apply to your property. Public nuisance laws may affect its upkeep and maintenance. Municipalities may exercise "eminent domain" and turn the use of your private property to common good. Because of this "shared ownership" notion, financial wealth as represented by private ownership of property may benefit private individuals and families, but its value and improvements may benefit the community, as well. The efforts of private property owners to respond responsibly to the shared ownership notion is usually looked upon with approval by society.

(2) **Genuine wealth increases personal opportunity.** Just as a machine may extend your physical ability with added horsepower, or a computer may extend your mental "horsepower," ownership of capital can extend the scope and richness of your life. The value of wealth may be exchanged for value in the form of possessions or other kinds of "property" or opportunities for self-expression or achievement.

(3) **Wealth can be passed on.** Inheritance laws may allow you as an owner of property to pass its value along to those who succeed you. Maintaining or improving the value of property to benefit succeeding generations is regarded by many as a "responsible" thing to do. In the process, it improves the common good.

Establishing and maintaining a good savings program is one of the fundamental paving stones on the road to financial freedom. There are two important factors involved in the accumulation and improvement or increase of your capital. The first is the development of a good savings plan, and the second is having a workable investment program.

Part of becoming financially free and, coincidentally, a responsible financial steward is saving with foresight and patience. Whether you are putting money aside for your own or your children's schooling, a dreamed-of vacation, a new home, your retirement, or just preparing for a "rainy day," savings involves looking toward the future. It is the fruit of planning ahead. In another sense, it is the economic form of postponed gratification. Its opposite is the "instant gratification" that has come to mark so much of our way of life in the last half of the 20th century.

It is not possible to over-emphasize the value and importance of consistent saving. Effective saving requires focus and consistency. If you were to pour a large bucket of water over a piece of sandstone every half hour for a period of ten years, very little would happen to the stone. However, if you were to let water drip on a certain point on the stone every second, minute by minute, hour by hour, for the same ten years it could work a noticeable indentation, perhaps even work its way entirely through the stone. There is great power in focus and consistency.

Saving can be a difficult habit to develop. Throughout our lives we are taught to spend. Advertisers invest hundreds of millions of dollars every year to promote worry-free spending by individuals of all ages, especially children. The very term **consumer**, which is commonly used to describe individual citizens, is a part of this overall attitude manipulation strategy.

Our entire culture downplays the importance of savings. Today, in an age of easy credit, many people are encouraged to spend now and pay later and "let tomorrow take care of itself." Typical of this attitude is the popular bumper sticker seen on many recreational vehicles belonging to retirees: "I'm spending my kids' inheritance."

The power of modern-day advertising is very compelling. The seductive forces that are at work in our modern world to influence us toward short-term buying decisions are very persuasive. The multi-billion-dollar advertising industry flourishes by glamorizing the "benefits" of instant gratification.

In a world of conveniences and instant gratification, it is far too easy for many people to take the path of least resistance, the "easy" road, the one that leads nowhere beyond today. Our grandparents dreamed of a world of tomorrow where much of the drudgery of earning a living would be taken over by machines and scientific wonders. They dreamed of thirty-hour work weeks, extended leisure time, and idyllic peace and prosperity. Now, that tomorrow is here, but not as they imagined it. Instead, many of us have become virtual slaves to its wonders and the notion of instant gratification it presents to us. Now, we work longer work weeks, have less and less time for leisure, and are chasing prosperity as if we were tied to the caboose of a runaway train. Often, we exercise too little choice in how we spend our money. We become financial slaves because we lack the self-discipline to make sound financial decisions.

Today, we seem much more interested in "things" than in "principles." Typical of this is the greater emphasis we place on the improved value of property rather than the pure value of land. The small parcels of "property" that many of today's landowners control, with the improvement of a house built on the land, is much different than the larger, more inherently productive tracts of land typical of land ownership in earlier times. Such fragile and all-too-temporary "improvements" represent our contemporary interest in "things" of limited duration. The emphasis is on the disposable rather than on enduring quality. This attitude expresses itself in a shortsightedness that causes us to devalue the virtues of planning for a long-term tomorrow.

The key to becoming a better saver is to learn new habits and attitudes regarding money and its use. Many of the most significant habits and attitudes you need have been discussed over the course of this book. Financial fitness places tremendous emphasis on long-term planning, on developing a living attitude that looks forward with confidence rather than being influenced by every immediate twist of fortune. Throughout this book you have been challenged to take responsibility for your financial future, and you have been shown how to develop a healthy financial philosophy that can lead you to a destination of financial independence and freedom.

It is of paramount importance to develop and apply an investment plan for your present as well as your future. The earlier in life you realize this the better. In fact, if you have children, teaching them the concept of *investment and return* is one of the most important and valuable gifts you can ever give them.

As your financial fitness plan enhances your financial freedom, you will be faced with the often times confusing challenge of where to invest your capital. Here are three tests to apply that will help you evaluate your options:

- **How useful will a particular investment be in enhancing my immediate quality of life, today and tomorrow?** Investment in personal assets can drastically affect this question. Such investments as your home or homes, primary and secondary residences, furnishings, automobiles, apparel, jewelry, and so forth, are important "personal" assets that may be considered as investments. Investing in land for personal agricultural use to raise your food, or investing in your own business to provide your livelihood, will affect this question, as well.
- **How secure is a particular investment or investment strategy?** Does your "portfolio," or collection and mix of investments, permit you to take heightened risk with a particular investment? Or do your circumstances and investment goals require a more conservative, security-oriented approach?
- **How can I best transact a particular investment, in the context of others, to optimize my involvement and return on capital?** Does this particular investment "make sense" in terms of your knowledge and experience? Does it fit your investment plans and satisfy your short- and long-term investment goals?

Here is a "menu" of investment options for you to consider as you prepare to define investment goals and plans. This menu, called the Responsible Financial Steward Investment Goal Sheet, on page 179 outlines investment opportunities that will assist you in planning short- and long-term goals and strategies.

RESPONSIBLE FINANCIAL STEWARD INVESTMENT GOAL SHEET			
INVESTMENTS	**ONE-YEAR PLAN $**	**FIVE-YEAR PLAN $**	**LIFETIME PLAN $**
PERSONAL ASSETS			
Home			
Furnishings			
Automobiles			
Apparel			
Jewelry			
INSURANCE			
Life insurance			
Health insurance			
Liability insurance			
Disaster insurance			
Business insurance			
Self-insurance			
REAL ESTATE			
Raw land			
Farm land			
Rental housing			
Commercial real estate			
YOUR OWN BUSINESS			
Business #1			
Business #2			
SOMEONE ELSE'S BUSINESS			
Stocks			
Mutual Funds			
MONEY MARKET			
Bonds			
Notes			
Loans			
Annuities			
TANGIBLES			
Metals			
Diamonds			
Art objects			
Collectibles			
Others			

- Your life's purpose
- Personal assets: home(s), furnishings, automobiles, apparel, jewelry.
- Insurance: life, health, liability, disaster, business, self-insurance.
- Real estate: raw land, farm land, rental housing, commercial real estate.
- Your own business.
- Someone else's business: stocks, mutual funds.
- Bonds, notes, loans, annuities.
- Gold, diamonds, art objects, collectibles.

As you consider these various investment opportunities, one factor will always accompany any choice you make: The future is uncertain. Each investment opportunity brings with it an element of uncertainty. Will the economy grow at a vigorous rate or falter in the face of difficulties? Will stocks rise to new heights or fall? Will interest rates go up or down? Will interest in collectibles or art be faddish or enduring?

Regardless of your answers to these uncertainty questions, some things are more certain. You must have a place to live; children's education may need to be financed; retirement awaits over the horizon, however distant that horizon may be or seem to be; and taxes need to be paid. These are just a few of life's more pressing imperatives that move us toward savings and investments.

It is important to understand that shifts in economic growth and interest, and fluctuations in financial markets, are normal parts of our nation's business and social cycles. These shifts and fluctuations have happened before, and they will happen again. Novel or cataclysmic economic events, such as sudden shifts in the financial markets, usually receive considerable media attention, but long-term success stories seldom receive the same kind of coverage. Do not be fooled by publicity. Consider the averages and the long term.

As you work on learning how to develop a long-term investment plan, remember that "**if you fail to plan, then you plan to fail.**" This adage applies to investment goals and strategies. Haphazard or poorly conceived investments may bring frustration and financial ruin. Years of budgets, savings, and self-discipline in your financial affairs can be put to naught by a failed, careless investment. To avoid such dismal prospects, and to assist you in your planning for functional financial fitness, we recommend the following three steps:

(1) **Define your investment objectives.** Everyone's financial needs are different. Yours are no exception. In order to define your investment goals and strategies, you need to ask yourself three questions about what your needs are:

(a) How does your investment plan support your life's purpose?

(b) What do you want from your investment? If you are young, you may want to invest to satisfy several goals such as a child's education, purchase of a home, a business of your own. If you are older, you may be looking toward retirement with its special capital needs. The goals you are seeking may be as varied as the many lifestyles that move people, but whatever they are, you need to identify them as best you can for the short term and for the long term.

(c) What is your investment horizon? When will you need the money that your investment capital is going to earn? Will you need it in five years, ten, twenty, fifty?

(2) **Know your limits for investment risk.** There is a basic rule that usually applies to all good investments: *"The greater the risk, the greater potential for reward."* If this rule does not hold true, it is not a good investment from the outset: If the return is not commensurate with the risk of the investment, avoid it at all cost. Of course, if you can find an investment with limited risk and great potential for reward, consider it by all means. Two questions that you might ask yourself about your investment risk limits are

(a) Are you comfortable risking some of your principal for a potentially greater reward?

(b) Would you rather accept a lower return as a trade-off for greater security or safety for your investment resources?

Your age can be a factor in determining your investment risk limits. Generally, the more distant your investment horizon, the greater risk you can be willing to accept. For example, if you are young and able to continue an investment for a reasonably long time, you may be more comfortable with the higher risks associated with certain more aggressive investments. However, if you are older or are nearing retirement, more conservative and secure investments may be better suited to your needs Only you can determine how safe "safe" is, but you must decide in order to have workable, and hopefully profitable, short- and long-term investment goals and strategies.

(3) **Build an investment portfolio that fits your objectives and risk limits.** Your investment portfolio is the collection or mix of investments you have made or are planning to make. No one mix of investments is ideal for everyone. Your plans should include building a portfolio that will fit your individual needs based on your objectives and risk limits. You may be investing for several goals simultaneously; your portfolio will reflect this.

Make your investment plans flexible enough that they can be modified when your investment needs change. Your portfolio can be structured and restructured to satisfy changing investment goals. Also, when constructing your portfolio, it is good to consider your savings for such things as ready-cash needs and assets to be used for emergencies.

A WORKABLE PLAN FOR INVESTMENT

Once you have defined your investment goals or objectives and determined your risk limits, you can begin to make investments and build your investment portfolio. These elements form your investment plan. The purpose of your plan is to optimize and maximize your investment success. The following plan may help you do that.

- People who make consist contributions to their church or other worthy causes are often more successful financially that those who do not. We encourage you to make it part of your plan.

- List savings as one of your committed objectives. However large or small the amount you have committed to savings, make it part of your financial plan. It will be a great habit to form.

Your Investment Account

A major milestone in your financial fitness training is the moment when you have obtained the financial freedom to be able to write a check to your own "investment" account as you pay your monthly bills. A "fast track" way to reach this point of financial health is to arrange to have the appropriate amount transferred automatically from your checking account into your investment account through automatic funds transfer or bank drafts.

Investing a fixed amount at regular intervals is called *dollar-cost averaging*. It is a simple strategy to help reduce investment risk. Your investment buys more value when the price is low and less value when the price is high. By spreading the investment over low- and high-price periods, it may accumulate at a lower average cost than if you had made the investment all at once at a single, perhaps higher, price. Of course, dollar-cost-averaging does not protect against a loss in declining markets. Such a possibility places a premium on continuing your investment for a longer term so that possible fluctuations in investment prices can average to your advantage and gain.

Diversify your investments to help reduce risk. Having a diversified investment program is smart. It leaves you less vulnerable to a major decline in any one investment, market, or industry. When investment markets are volatile and fluctuating, some investments may lose value while others may realize significant gains.

For example, if you own stocks, bonds, and money market instruments, you won't be as vulnerable to a decline in the stock market as an investor who owns only stocks. If you invest in gold, fine art, and collectibles, you won't be as exposed as you would be if you just invested in gold alone.

A word of caution, however, regarding mutual funds. Sometimes investors suppose that they have sufficiently diversified their investments by investing in a mutual fund. Such a fund often diversifies its investments as a hedge against risk. However, as an investor in such a fund, all of your risk is channeled through this one fund, and you may be vulnerable to fund mismanagement or administrative peculiarities.

Keep in mind that no single investment can fit all your needs through every phase of your life. That is why it is important to create a flexible, diversified investment program that can be modified as you grow older or your needs change.

Next time you go for a walk, pick up a twig and break it in half using both hands. It won't be difficult. Then try holding about a dozen twigs of similar size in a bundle and breaking them in half with both hands. You will find this to be far more difficult. The same philosophy should guide your investment portfolio. If all your investment is concentrated in one twig, your entire investment program could be "broken" if something goes wrong. However, by spreading your investment assets among many investments, you have a "strong" position that protects you in case of reverses.

Reinvest your earnings. Depending upon your investment horizon for a particular investment, you may find that you really do not need to use the income it generates. If you find that you do not, you can put the income back to work by reinvesting it. Often this can be done immediately and automatically.

For example, most mutual funds allow you to reinvest dividends or capital gains distributions automatically. When you reinvest in this manner, you increase the opportunity for greater return.

Remember the power of compound interest and "the rule of 72" we discussed earlier? This rule also applies to how your investment will double when earnings are reinvested: the rate of doubling is projected by dividing 72 by the annual rate of return. For example, at an 8% annual growth rate, your investment will double every nine years if earnings are reinvested.

Maintain a long-term perspective with your investment program. With investing, patience may be all important. Over the short term, financial markets rise and fall in response to many diverse factors. Attempting to anticipate these market fluctuations for quick gains is extremely perilous. Most successful investors take the long-term approach to pursuing their investment goals and objectives.

Now, here are some suggestions for a *financial fitness recipe for investment.*

(1) Make only modest investments in those personal assets that do not provide any return or financial appreciation.
(2) Develop a solid insurance program.
(3) Pick one or, at most, two areas of investment for a major return and stay within those areas during your investment lifetime.
(4) Make all investments for the long term, but take a loss and start over if the long-term situation changes.
(5) Diversify investments within your chosen areas.
(6) Study and work with others. Develop a sense of intuition about your chosen areas. Continue to improve your understanding of factors that can affect your investments.

The greatest investment you can make is the investment of your life. How you choose to invest it is up to you. If you build on what you have learned in this book you will be investing your life in a worthwhile cause - regaining your American heritage of financial fitness.

CHAPTER ELEVEN

A Uniquely American Heritage

For many of you this last chapter of the book is the end. For those of you who have been struck by the chord of relevance and hope that this book offers, your story has only begun. For you this closing chapter will actually become the beginning of a journey towards an entirely new and fulfilling life of financial fitness and financial freedom.

This book describes a series of exercises based upon a particular philosophical stance about the meaning and purpose of life. This stance and these financial exercises are grounded in firm and sound spiritual, mental, emotional, volitional, and physical principles and practices that if adopted and applied diligently, will change your life forever.

FINANCIAL FITNESS FACT # 11

"In God We Trust"

We all share a common desire for success. Success has a different meaning for each of us. But one thing is common to all truly successful endeavors. That commonality is the sense of happiness, satisfaction, and fulfillment that occurs whenever we achieve the goals we set out to accomplish. This is particularly true in the financial aspects of our lives.

With this book we are offering a guide for achieving financial fitness and freedom. This book can direct you towards a process for achieving financial success. Now, by this we don't just mean the accumulation of wealth and goods. We believe that the pursuit of material things at the expense of quality living experiences is a primary reason why so many Americans lose, or risk losing, a distinct part of their heritage – their financial freedom. The accumulation of wealth and financial freedom is of little significance compared to the *joy of knowing that while one is growing in material possessions, inner growth and development is also occurring*. The greatest aspect of success is the feeling of self-fulfillment and contentment in knowing not only that you can survive financially under any circumstances but that you can survive - even thrive - spiritually and emotionally as well. This is the kind of success the principles discussed in this book can help you achieve..

It requires courage to face financial realities and to take the steps necessary to become financially fit. Most people say that they would like to be debt-free, but often they are not willing to take the first steps. Beginning the journey is often the hardest thing to do. It requires an act of will. It is like waking up to a whole new way of living your life. Change and improvement will come no other way. Those people are well on their way to success who say, "I *will* be debt free," and then begin the journey by committing themselves to learning and applying the principles of financial discipline that we have described throughout this book. Our greatest hope is that we have in some manner stirred within you a burning desire to change your life, to improve the quality of opportunities for yourself and your loved ones.

The first step is committing yourself to the journey ahead.

The second step is realizing that you will have to make changes. Financial freedom can be realized only when life-changing decisions are made and resolutely pursued. Change is something that we often talk about, but only a few of us make the sacrifices needed to change our lives for the better. Ask yourself if you are content with your role as a *consumer*, or do you think that there is more to be gained from your God-given time on this earth than the mere pursuit and acquisition of material goods? Only if you are capable of accepting the ideals of a *higher purpose to life* can you hope to achieve true financial freedom The principles described in this book have proven to be very effective, but you must first want them for yourself, have faith, and exercise your ability to achieve the life-changing habits and attitudes that financial fitness and freedom represent. Wishful thinking will get you nowhere. If you desire to change your life, you must make these principles a living part of you. To do this, you must commit your total being, your spiritual, mental, emotional, volitional, and physical self to the life-changing decisions and efforts *Wake Up, America* has set before you. There will be no "quick fix" solutions. You must believe and accept that the journey can be completed successfully and happily.

Reading this book and applying the principles it reveals is the first step in your journey towards a once-in-a-lifetime opportunity to change, then grab the opportunity to live a complete and fulfilling life, a life filled with meaning, joy, purpose, and happiness.

Finally, our American heritage is solidly founded on a spiritual tradition that yields life-directing qualities that include, faith, wisdom, and purpose. A life guided by and lived within the boundaries of these qualities leads to emotions, attitudes, values, and behaviors consistent with freedom in all areas of life, including finances.

Our American heritage is built on a specific view of wisdom as expressed in our Declaration of Independence, Bill of Rights, and Constitution. For example, our Declaration of Independence states that we are endowed by our Creator with certain inalienable rights. America is built on this foundation of an unrelenting faith and belief in the concept of inalienable rights endowed by our Creator. Even our money acknowledges, *"In God We Trust."*

To the degree our nation has honored these rights, we have prospered in freedom. On the other hand, in whatever area of life we have deviated from these rights, we have experienced loss of freedom, deterioration of quality of life, violence, and even bondage to debt. As we each learn to regain our American heritage of freedom from debt, our nation will again become debt free and, guided by the principles of our spiritual tradition, we will be able to pursue our individual and national destiny.

We want to welcome you to the journey towards a new and fulfilling chapter in your life. This book should be seen as a beacon of hope lighting your way to financial health, freedom, and responsibility. The Financial Fitness Centers located throughout the United States stand ready to join with you on your journey towards success and happiness. If you feel you are ready to begin living your new financial life now and would like additional help or guidance, the Financial Fitness Centers are available to serve you. The *Wake Up, America* call you have heard in this book is aimed at you. Because each one of us is America. Our country is the sum total of the experiences of all of her people. So listen carefully. That sound you are hearing is your name being called. Wake Up! Regain your American heritage of financial freedom. Start living your life the way it was meant to be lived. Don't let anything stand in your way. *God Bless America.*

NEED MORE MATERIALS?

All of the materials in this book can be ordered from Financial Freedom Enterprises

---

Financial Fitness Budget Worksheet

Financial Fitness Creditor Summary Sheet

Financial Fitness Centers – Toy Inventory Sheet

Mr. Money Financial Planner for Children

BluePrint Budget Register®

Financial Freedom Enterprises
180 North Woodruff
Idaho Falls, ID 83403

1-800-669-8815

Call today
for more
information
and pricing
or to locate the
Financial Fitness Center
nearest you.

REFERENCES

The data collected in this book was obtained by Carol Walker from the following publications:

Ken Kunsman & Charles A. Jaffe
The Morning Call Newspaper
Sunday, October 10, 1993
Philadelphia, PA

Thomas McCarroll, Carry That Weight
Time Magazine
November 19, 1990

David Stockman, No East Cure for Read Ink
US News & World Report
May 6, 1991

Earl Ubell & Carol C. Flax
Does Money Control Your Life?
Parade Magazine
October 28, 1990

Martin Burns, Banks Must Lend or Die
Loans Must Be Repaid
Spotlight on Finance
Spotlight, January 21, 1991

Janice Catro, Charge It Your Way
Time Magazine
July 1, 1991

Eva Pomice & Dana Hawkins, The New Fear Of buying
US News & World Report
March 4, 1991

Bernie Ward, The Decade of the Child
Sky Magazine
June 1991

The Washington Post
National Weekly Edition
Bringing Down the House of Cards
October 28 - November 4, 1990

Personal Finance
Jerome B. Cohen and Arthur Hanson
Richard D. Irwin Inc.
Homewood, Illinois

Day of Reckoning
Benjamin M. Friedman
Random House New York

Regions of Opportunity
Jack Lessinger, Ph.D.
Times Books

Personal Finance
E. Thomas Garman & Raymond E. Forgue
Houghton Mifflin Company

Kiplinger's Personal Finance Magazine
March 1993

Here's When We Will Feel Better
Money Magazine
Forecast 1993

A Better Way to Insure Your Senior Years
Business Week
June 7, 1993

Gerri Detweiler
Controlling Your Credit Union Plus
Summer, 1994

John Greenwald, A Slump That Won't Go Away
Time Magazine
October 14, 1991

Marc, Levinson, Living On the Edge
Newsweek
November 4, 1991

Robert F. Black, Heavy Lifting
US News & World Report
May 6, 1991

Aaron Bernstein, What Happened to the American Dream
Business Week
August 19, 1991

Charlotte Allen, The Bankruptcy Boom
Insight Magazine
June 24, 1991

The McAlvany Intelligence Advisor
The Economy - The Stage is Set for Disaster
November, 1989

Janice, Castro, Hunkering Down
Time Magazine
July 23, 1990

Beth Kobliner, Tight Times for 20 Somethings
Money Magazine
August, 1991

Healthy Menus Lighten the Road
Cooking Light
March/April 1993

Consumer Economic Issues In America
Edition 2.5
E. Thomas Garman
Dame Publication, Inc.

Consumer Information Center
Pueblo, Colorado 81009

Department of Health & Human Services
5600 Fishers Lane
Rockville, MD 20857

US Office of Consumer Affairs
1725 I Street, NW, Suite 1009
Washington, DC 20206

Mortimer B. Zuckerman
This is a Thrift Industry?
US News & World Report
August 6, 1990

James K. Glassman
The U.S. Banking System is All Better - or Maybe Not
The Washington Post
June 1, 1994

H. Rowan, Savings & Loan Crisis
The Washington Post
October 22, 1989

George Will, Nothing Inevitable About S&L Mess
Roanoke Time & News-World

How to Teach Children About Money
Young American Bank
Denver, Colorado

Mortimer B. Zukerman, The Wages of Debt
US News & World Report
April 15, 1991

Mortimer B. Zukerman, The Free Ride is Over
US News & World Report
October 15, 1990

Thomas McCarroll, Hitting the Credit Limit
Time Magazine
September 9, 1991

John Greenwald, Crawling Out Of The Slump
Time Magazine
June 17, 1991

Crunched By Credit
The Economist
November 3-9, 1990

David Hage, Taking air Out of the Recovery
US News & World Report
August 3, 1992

Howard Rudnitsky, An Excess of Plastic
Forbes Magazine
February 4, 1991

America's New Debt Wagon
The Economist
December 1, 1990

Federal Reserve Bank of New York
Public Information Department
33 Liberty Street
New York, New York 10045

Statistical Abstract of the United States, 1994

National Institute for Consumer Education
College of Education
Eastern Michigan University
Ypsilanti, Michigan 48197

American Association of Retired Persons
601 E Street, NW
Washington, D.C. 20049

Peter Newcomb, Hey, Dude, Let's Consume
Forbes Magazine
June 11, 1990